THE REDEMPTION OF SCROOGE

The Redemption of Scrooge

The Redemption of Scrooge
978-1-5018-2307-7
978-1-5018-2308-4 eBook

The Redemption of Scrooge: Leader Guide
978-1-5018-2309-1
978-1-5018-2310-7 eBook

The Redemption of Scrooge: DVD
978-1-5018-2311-4

The Redemption of Scrooge: Youth Study Book
978-1-5018-2316-9
978-1-5018-2317-6 eBook

The Redemption of Scrooge: Worship Resources
978-1-5018-2320-6 Flash Drive
978-1-5018-2321-3 Download

Also by Matt Rawle

The Faith of a Mockingbird

The Salvation of Doctor Who

Hollywood Jesus

For more information, visit MattRawle.com.

MATT RAWLE

The Redemption of Scrooge

Abingdon Press / Nashville

The Redemption of Scrooge

Copyright © 2016 by Abingdon Press
All rights reserved.

This book is printed on elemental chlorine-free paper.
Library of Congress Cataloging-in-Publication data applied for.
ISBN 978-1-5018-2307-7

16 17 18 19 20 21 22 23 24 25—10 9 8 7 6 5 4 3 2
MANUFACTURED IN THE UNITED STATES OF AMERICA

To my new baby boy, Robert Thomas Rawle

CONTENTS

linked with all of the other elements that are so ever-present and familiar during the holiday season—neither the Advent wreath nor Santa Claus has seen much change over the years.

Charles Dickens's classic story *A Christmas Carol* was originally titled *A Christmas Carol in Prose, Being a Ghost Story of Christmas*—a curious title to say the least. Dickens's story is not a song, though like a traditional carol, it is divided into staves, or verses, with each section offering an independent thought. There are many variations for the definition of a carol, but I particularly like the one that defines *carol* as "an old round dance with singing."[1] Just like a circle has no beginning and no end, the carols of our faith seem timeless. Perhaps Dickens wanted his story to be shared over and over again, year after year, like a familiar carol, in order to bring people together in joy.

A Christmas Carol, however, is not your traditional Christmas story. The story begins with "Marley was dead" (Dickens, *A Christmas Carol*, Stave One), a rather unconventional way to welcome the holiday season, don't you think? (I mean, what goes better with Christmas than creepy ghosts, right?) But, by the end of Ebenezer Scrooge's journey, we find that Scrooge has found new life. And so, as odd as it may seem to start a Christmas story with death, by the end, it all makes perfect sense. At the beginning of the story, on Christmas Eve, Scrooge is just as good as dead—his soul is as frigid as the bleak midwinter air. He goes on a difficult and frightful journey, and eventually wakes up on Christmas morning a changed man.

A Christmas Carol is a timeless story, not only because we hear about Scrooge's past, present, and future, but because generations have told and retold this story in their own way. Just as a new artist interprets a two-hundred-year-old carol in a new key, *A Christmas Carol* has seen many adaptations through the years. From community theater stage to silent films, from Mickey Mouse to 3-D computer animated motion capture, *A Christmas Carol* is a tale of redemption that will be with us for a long time to come! It is a story that has embedded itself into our culture and, for many of us, has become a routine fixture in our holiday traditions. Everyone knows what is means to be called a *Scrooge*, and poor little Tiny Tim still has the ability to pull on our heartstrings. For over a hundred years now, *A Christmas Carol* has been a part of our pop culture.

THE POP IN CULTURE

What comes to mind when you hear someone refer to *pop culture*? Sometimes when we think of pop culture, words like *cutting edge* or *current* come to mind, but this is certainly not the case for Christmas. Most of our modern-day cultural expressions during the holiday season are rooted in traditions from hundreds of years ago, and revolve around a story two thousand years old.

Regardless if you think an example of pop culture is the latest pop Christmas song on iTunes or something more edgy like *The Walking Dead*, there's no denying that the popular music, books, television, movies, and media have much to say about the world in which we live. The word *culture* is used often, by many different people in many different ways, but in its simplest form, *culture* is simply an expression of how a community understands itself. God, our Creator, supplies us with the raw ingredients of humanity—talents, time, creativity, desires, ingenuity—and "culture" is whatever we cook up. Stories, songs, recipes, traditions, art, and language are all displays of how we interpret the world and our place in it.

So what role does God play in our culture—in our day-to-day lives and in the work of our hands, which produces music and art and literature and plays and movies and technology? Throughout history, people have debated this issue and adamantly drawn a dividing line between that which should be considered "sacred" (that which is explicitly religious in nature) and that which should be considered "secular" (that is, everything else). At first glance, these may be seemingly easy judgments to make, but when we stop to examine what God has to say about this division, we might be surprised at what we find.

Scripture says that *all* things were made through Christ (John 1:3), and through Christ *all* things were reconciled to God (Colossians 1:20). In other words, everything and everyone in our world contains a spark of the divine—everything is sacred, and whether or not we choose to live in that truth depends on our perspective. For example, think of sunlight as a holy (sacred) gift from God. God offers us sunlight so we can see the world around us. We can celebrate the sacred by creating things that enhance the light in our homes, such as larger windows or skylights, or we can hang heavy drapes and close the shutters in order to diminish the sacred and shut out the light. Our sacred work is letting in as much light as possible, and those things that keep the light out need to be rejected or transformed.

Through Jesus, God put on flesh and walked among us, in our world, in order to re-narrate what it means to be a child of God. God assumed culture and transformed it. So now all is sacred, and in everything we are to see and proclaim his glory. I truly believe we are called not to reject the culture we live in, but to re-narrate its meaning—to tell God's story in the midst of it. Jesus didn't reject the cross (the sin of our world); rather, Jesus accepted it and transformed it from a death instrument into a symbol of life and reconciliation.

Sometimes it's easy to see God in the midst of culture—in the stories of Scripture and in reverent hymns and worshipful icons. *A Christmas Carol* is one of those stories that preaches the gospel pretty clearly, I think. But other times the divine is more veiled—hidden in a novel, concealed in classic rock, obscured by an impressionist's palate. That is why we created this Pop in Culture series, a collection of studies about faith and popular culture. Each study uses a work of pop culture as a way to examine questions and issues of the Christian faith. Our hope and prayer is that the studies will open our eyes to the spiritual truths that exist all around us in books, movies, music, and television.

As we walk with Christ, we discover the divine all around us, and in turn, the world invites us into a deeper picture of its Creator. Through this lens of God's redemption story, we are invited to look at culture in a new and inviting way. We are invited to dive into the realms of literature, art, and entertainment to explore and discover how God is working in and through us and in the world around us to tell his great story of redemption. And if Scrooge can be redeemed, then so can we!

A CHRISTMAS CAROL

A QUICK REFRESHER

Charles Dickens's classic *A Christmas Carol*, first published in 1843, begins on an ominous note, stating the fact that "Marley was dead: to begin with" (Stave One). The story takes place on Christmas Eve, Ebenezer Scrooge's least favorite time of the year. He glares at carolers and scolds his employee, Bob Cratchit, before turning down his nephew's invitation to Christmas dinner.

Arriving home, Scrooge is startled to find the ghostly face of Jacob Marley staring at him from the door knocker. It disappears, but soon he hears sounds like chains dragging on the floor. They creep closer and closer, until Jacob Marley appears as a ghostly apparition. He warns Scrooge that he must change his ways and that three ghosts will visit Scrooge over the next three days, offering him a chance at redemption from his awful fate.

Scrooge settles into his bed, thinking it all a horrible dream, but soon a bright light disturbs him. It is the Ghost of Christmas Past.

The spirit transports Scrooge to his childhood hometown, where he is reminded of childhood loneliness, adolescent joy, and the pain of unrequited love. Scrooge, upset, takes the extinguisher-cap and tries to eliminate the ghost's light. He ends up back in his room and falls into a deep sleep.

Scrooge is awakened when the clock strikes one. He ventures to the adjacent room to see the Ghost of Christmas Present, who transports Scrooge to a dingy corner of London where, despite their surroundings, the people are filled with Christmas cheer. The ghost brings him to the home of his clerk, Bob Cratchit, where Bob's son Tiny Tim tugs at Scrooge's heartstrings. Scrooge's journey continues to the home of his nephew, Fred, who proclaims that he will continue to invite the bad-tempered Scrooge to Christmas dinner every year. As they leave the scene, Scrooge notices that the ghost is aging rapidly. The ghost's life will end that night, but not before Scrooge notices two children hidden beneath the ghost's robes—a boy and a girl, dirty, with hands like claws. When Scrooge asks where their shelter is, the ghost repeats Scrooge's earlier words: "Are there no prisons? . . . Are there no workhouses?" (Stave One).

With that, the bell strikes twelve, and the Ghost of Christmas Present is gone, replaced by a draped phantom moving toward Scrooge. This ghost is silent and only responds with a pointed skeletal finger when asked if he is the Ghost of Christmas Yet to Come. Scrooge is transported to depressing scenes foreshadowing his own demise. The scene moves to the Cratchits' home, where the once jolly family is now morose. Tim has died, and Bob has just returned from his grave, telling his wife how lovely and green a place it is. Scrooge, distraught from seeing his own grave, exclaims that he will change his ways and live with the spirit of Christmas in his heart in order to change this future. The ghost shrinks away, and Scrooge finds himself back in his familiar bedroom.

Indeed, after these visits, Scrooge wakes the next morning full of the Christmas spirit. He runs from the house, filled with the joy of the season, and is surprised and grateful to discover that he hasn't missed Christmas Day. Scrooge makes good on his promise, becoming like a second father to Tiny Tim, and a good friend, master, and man to the city he once scorned. It was said thereafter that he "knew how to keep Christmas well." The story ends with Tiny Tim's famous words: "God bless Us, Every One!" (Stave Five).

CHAPTER ONE

BAH! HUMBUG!

But he was a tight-fisted hand at the grind-stone,
Scrooge! a squeezing, wrenching, grasping, scraping,
clutching, covetous, old sinner! (Stave One)

The dismissive response, "Bah! Humbug!" perfectly expresses the worldview of Ebenezer Scrooge, the tragic main character of Charles Dickens's *A Christmas Carol*. Scrooge is a sad man, and Christmas is not a happy time for him; but to be fair, no time during the year seems to bring Scrooge much joy. Since its original publication in 1843, *A Christmas Carol* has been presented often and in many very different ways. For example, this classic ghost story has been a mainstay in movie theaters, ranging from the 1901 *Scrooge, or, Marley's Ghost* silent film to *Mickey's Christmas Carol* (1983), to Disney's latest 2009 film adaptation starring Jim Carrey. Even though these versions of Scrooge's story are quite different, Scrooge the character remains consistent. In a way, Scrooge has taken on a life of his own, independent of Dickens's original story.

Scrooge is an iconic figure who represents stinginess, greed, and generally being in a terrible mood. If Scrooge can be redeemed, then so can we.

Scrooge is an iconic figure who represents stinginess, greed, and generally being in a terrible mood. Testament to the negative image his name implies, there were only twelve children in England named Ebenezer in 2013.[1] Interestingly, though, "Ebenezer" is a Hebrew word meaning, "stone of help" (see 1 Samuel 7:12). Maybe you remember singing about it in the second stanza of "Come, Thou Fount of Every Blessing": "Here I raise mine Ebenezer; hither by thy help I'm come."[2] Even though by the end of the story Ebenezer Scrooge is a changed person, the character remains a strong caricature of everything our Christmas celebrations shouldn't be. It seems that we can't accept that he has been redeemed. But maybe there's still hope. Maybe over the course of this study, even Ebenezer Scrooge's name might come to mean something different to you. After all, if Scrooge can be redeemed, then so can we.

MARLEY WAS DEAD

Marley was dead: to begin with. There is no doubt whatever about that. (Stave One)

"Marley was dead" seems like an unusual beginning for a Christmas story, but then again, Charles Dickens's *A Christmas Carol* is not your typical Christmas story—it is an unconventional hero's tale.

An anonymous narrator offers us a window into the world of the miser Ebenezer Scrooge—a name that has become synonymous with being grumpy, bitter, angry, or less-than-enthused about the holiday season. Through the tale of Scrooge, an old man whom Dickens describes as "a squeezing, wrenching, grasping, scraping, clutching, covetous, old sinner," we are taken on an unlikely adventure (Stave One). On a cold Christmas Eve night, Scrooge encounters three spirits who reveal his past, his present, and his future in the hope of transforming a covetous old sinner's heart.

But before we embark on a supernatural noel, Dickens wants to make sure we know the facts. Marley, Scrooge's longtime business partner, is dead. The story must begin with the fact that Marley is dead; otherwise the rest of the story makes little sense.

In order to understand the story, it's important to know the facts. Several years ago my family was having dinner with some friends, and my oldest daughter discovered that she quite enjoyed the candy corn our hosts were serving in the candy dishes. After noticing she had consumed several handfuls, we picked up the candy and told her she had had enough. Moments later, while the grown-ups were finishing our meal, we heard a crash in the living room. I ran in and saw an overturned, lit candle surrounded by shards of glass from a broken vase. Pieces of candy corn were everywhere, and the only soul in the room was my daughter. I looked at her with pursed lips, brow furrowed and arms crossed.

"What happened?!" she said, eyes wide.

"What do you mean, 'what happened?'" I snapped. "It looks like someone wanted to get some extra candy corn!"

ADVENT WEEK 1: PEACE

This week we light the candle of Peace. *Peace*, much like the word *past*, needs some qualifiers and context. Does being at peace mean that we are not fighting? Maybe things are peaceful because people are afraid to speak up out of fear. Maybe peace represents not raising your voice or entering a heated debate or everyone simply minding his or her own business, but this kind of peace looks more like apathy, which certainly isn't why we light candles during Advent.

Many names are used throughout Scripture to describe the person and work of Jesus—Wonderful Counselor, Mighty God, Eternal Father, and Prince of Peace (Isaiah 9:6) to name a few. Isaiah points to peace as one of the signs that God has offered the Messiah to God's people; but interestingly Jesus says in Matthew 10:34, "Don't think that I've come to bring peace to the earth. I haven't come to bring peace but a sword." This offers us a clue as to what kind of peace God desires. A godly peace goes beyond lack of fighting or reservation or apathy. Peace is mentioned at Jesus' birth when the angel said, "Don't be afraid, . . . Glory to God in heaven, and on earth peace among those whom he favors" (Luke 2:10, 14). Jesus, before his arrest and crucifixion, gathered his disciples together and said, "Peace I leave with you. My peace I give you. I give to you not as the world gives. Don't be troubled or afraid" (John 14:27). When Jesus was resurrected, he appeared to the disciples, who were hiding behind a locked door out of fear, and Jesus' first words to them were, "Peace be with you."

Peace is not lack of conflict. Following Jesus will result in quite a lot of conflict with the world. Jesus is the Prince of Peace because the peace he offers is the opposite of fear. We light the candle of Peace so that the light will burn away our fear of what following Christ might mean.

Gracious God, Father of the Prince of Peace, help us to follow where your light shines. Hope is the destination of our faith, and peace gives us the courage to start the journey. In the name of the Father and of the Son and of the Holy Spirit. Amen.

"Well, who did that?" my daughter had the gall to ask.

"Seriously?"

Then she started to weep melodramatically. "But father...I just love candy corn so much."

It didn't take Sherlock to understand the facts of the situation, but had we not heard the glass vase crashing to the floor, we wouldn't have caught her red-handed. If it had happened silently, our host would probably have discovered the mess later, wondering what in the world had happened.

Like I said, it's important to have all the pertinent facts in order to understand the story, and so Dickens wants us to know this important fact—*Marley was dead*—right from the very beginning. This statement sets the tone for the story and foreshadows what's to come. This setup makes me think very much about the Advent season. Advent, from the Latin word *ad venire*, means "to come."[3] The four Sundays before Christmas Day, the church gathers to wait for the Christ Child's birth. During this time we read stories from the Old Testament, in which God laid out the plan to send a Messiah to save God's people. The prophet Isaiah proclaims:

> A child is born to us, a son is given to us,
>> and authority will be on his shoulders.
>> He will be named
>> Wonderful Counselor, Mighty God,
>> Eternal Father, Prince of Peace.
> There will be vast authority and endless peace
>> for David's throne and for his kingdom,
>> establishing and sustaining it
>> with justice and righteousness
>> now and forever.
>
>> (Isaiah 9:6-7)

> A shoot shall come out from the stump of Jesse,
>> and a branch shall grow out of his roots.

21

The spirit of the LORD shall rest on him,
> the spirit of wisdom and understanding,
> the spirit of counsel and might,
> the spirit of knowledge and the fear of the LORD.

(Isaiah 11:1-2 NRSV)

During Advent, Christians sing songs such as, "O Come, O Come, Emmanuel" and "Come, Thou Long-Expected Jesus." These songs anticipate the hope that God's people felt as they waited for this Savior. Congregations light candles of hope, peace, love, and joy, like an emblazoned clock counting down to God's intervention. My family has an Advent calendar with hand-sewn Nativity story characters, which travel daily from numbered pocket to numbered pocket on a red and green felt background.

Waiting for something that has already happened is a curious practice. Explaining the season of Advent was quite difficult for me until my wife and I were pregnant with our first child. When a child is in the womb, the child is certainly real even though you can't hold the baby in your arms. A mother's body changes, subtle flutters soon become kicks, and ultrasounds reveal a profile, leading someone to say, "She looks just like you!" or "Are you sure you aren't having an alien?" The child is certainly real, but not yet born. It's kind of like recording kick counts as the baby's due date approaches. Ask any mother—the baby is already here, but not yet born.

The Advent season plays with our notion of time. The church gathers in the present to ponder the past for a future hope. *A Christmas Carol* is a beautiful story for the Advent season because it is a tale in which the past, present, and future all come together in one transformative night. Certainly this story is about Scrooge's love of money and his altruistic failures, but it is also a story about how Scrooge cannot let go of his past. Early in the story, after establishing that Marley had been dead for some time, Dickens writes, "Scrooge never painted out Old Marley's name. There it stood, years afterwards, above the warehouse door: Scrooge and Marley" (Stave One). Scrooge seems to cling to the past because his (only?) friend Marley represented the only things in which Scrooge trusts: hard work, frugality, unwavering discipline, and action that can be weighed, measured, and counted.

The Advent season plays with our notion of time. The church gathers in the present to ponder the past for a future hope.

One of the reasons I love the song "Lo, How a Rose E'er Blooming" is because it's difficult to count. The time signature is common time (four beats per measure and the quarter note gets the beat), but each measure seems to flow into the next without a structured beat or meter. Rarely does a phrase in the song begin with beat one, and words are extended past measure breaks. The song also talks about the promises of the past coming into fruition. The words and music together suggest that the past and future unite in an ambiguous but blessed present. Scrooge is stuck in the past, and he can't move forward because one can only count what one's already been given. If your world is only what can be weighed and measured, Advent's "here, but not yet" mantra makes too little sense for a merry investment.

Jesus came to save us from counting our past as our only reality. It's like when Moses led God's people out of Egyptian slavery into the wilderness. Before they reached the Promised Land, the Book of Exodus says, "The whole congregation of the Israelites complained against Moses and Aaron in the wilderness. The Israelites said to them, 'If only we had died by the hand of the LORD in the land of Egypt...for you have brought us out into this wilderness to kill this whole assembly with hunger'" (Exodus 16:2-3 NRSV). Because living in the wilderness was difficult and they were caught wandering between where they were and where they were heading, the people complained and wished they had died as slaves. The people became stubborn and bitter (see Exodus 32:9), almost "Scroogelike" in their relationship with God and one another. Instead of moving forward in faith, trusting that God was with them, the people kept looking over their shoulders, hopelessly lamenting over the way things were.

Advent is like living in the wilderness between what was and what will be. Living into this tension, remembering God's promises, and depending on faith become spiritual disciplines that keep us from becoming Scrooges ourselves. Even though the Promised Land may seem far off, we hold tightly to the promises of our God, for "he who promised is faithful" (Hebrews 10:23 NIV).

How have your Christmas traditions changed over time? What was it like when you first began a new tradition?

How does your community of faith celebrate Advent?

Read the lyrics from "Come, Thou Long-Expected Jesus." How might this hymn guide your worship during Advent?

SING WE NOW OF CHRISTMAS

"I wish to be left alone." (Stave One)

Long ago, when I first opened the book *A Christmas Carol*, I was surprised to find that it wasn't a songbook because the word *carol* usually refers to a religious folk song or Christmas hymn. Dickens's

Carol is no songbook, but it was certainly intended to invoke a reader's familiarity with Christmas songs since the story is organized into five staves, or stanzas, like a piece of music without musical notes. Why might that be?

Hymns and other religious songs are meant to communicate theology, tradition, and an experience of God. And, in large part, music is the vehicle through which theology and tradition and story is learned. Think back to preschool when you were learning your ABCs. Do you remember reciting the alphabet to the tune of "Twinkle, Twinkle, Little Star"? The only reason I can recite the Preamble of the Constitution is because of *Schoolhouse Rock!*, and I have to thank the *Animaniacs* for helping me memorize the state capitals ("Baton Rouge, Louisiana, Indianapolis, Indiana, and Columbus is the capital of Ohio…"). Even if one is relatively unfamiliar with the Christian tradition, he or she can probably still finish the lyric: "Hark! the herald angels sing, glory to _____" or "Silent night, _____ night." Much like songs help us remember important information, stories aid us in understanding meaning. Fables like *Little Red Riding Hood, Beauty and the Beast,* and the *Three Little Pigs* teach us important moral lessons in a memorable way. This is one of the reasons why Jesus spent so much time teaching through stories called parables. The "Prodigal Son" reminds us of God's grace, the "Good Samaritan" urges us to offer compassion, and "The Sheep and the Goats" cautions us against forgetting the sick, the hungry, and imprisoned. And though Dickens's "carol" is longer than a parable and isn't set to music, he uses the power of story to remind us that there is no soul too gruff, too cold, or too cantankerous for God's redeeming power.

An appropriate title for *A Christmas Carol* could be "In the Bleak Midwinter." This Christmas carol, based on Christina Rossetti's late-nineteenth-century poem, begins with a cold and barren landscape and ends with a heart offered to the Christ Child. Like the carol, Dickens's opening stave describes Scrooge with a desolate, apathetic slant—"No warmth could warm, no wintry weather chill him. No wind that blew was bitterer than he" (Stave One). Scrooge isn't completely unfeeling—he certainly cares about money. When you stare at a spreadsheet all day, making sure there is a zero balance at the end of the day, it gives you a peculiar view of life. For Scrooge, everything seems quantifiable. Scrooge's philosophy is grounded in "You reap what you sow," a manageable, balanced, and cultural mantra that takes one Scripture—Galatians 6:7—too far and out of context.

If "Make no mistake, God is not mocked. A person will harvest what they plant" (Galatians 6:7) is the sole foundation for our understanding of God, we run the risk of understanding salvation as a reward for ending life "in the black." First, "sin" isn't quantifiable. It is not the case that if you sin five times, you simply ask for forgiveness five times and you're covered. Instead, Scripture says, "For the wages of sin is death, but the free gift of God is eternal life in Christ Jesus our Lord" (Romans 6:23 NRSV), and "When you were dead in trespasses and the uncircumcision of your flesh, God made you alive together with him, when he forgave us all our trespasses, erasing the record that stood against us with its legal demands" (Colossians 2:13-14 NRSV). Taken out of context, this can make salvation sound like a gift card that simply covers the amount of sinful debt accrued. Salvation is not a savings account; rather salvation is a healing process that transforms who we are and conforms us into the image of Christ. In other words, salvation happens in a hospital, not a bank.

It's easy to see how salvation can be seen as a transaction. Every day we go to work, buy groceries, follow the stock market, give birthday presents, buy school supplies, and sell products. To say that Jesus "paid the debt" is not an altogether bad analogy, but when taken too far the gospel becomes a simple means of prosperity. When prosperity becomes the only measure of a godly life, the poor are vilified, the less fortunate are assumed to be lazy, greedy, and apathetic. Pastors only appoint big givers to church leadership, and mission work becomes something done for the poor rather than an invitation for the voiceless to speak. When asked if Scrooge would offer alms for the poor, he replied, "Are there no prisons?...I can't afford to make idle people merry. I help to support the establishments I have mentioned—they cost enough; and those who are badly off must to there" (Stave One).

Jesus' parable of the vineyard is shocking to our modern economic ears:

> "For the kingdom of heaven is like a landowner who went out early in the morning to hire laborers for his vineyard....But he replied to one of them, 'Friend, I am doing you no wrong; did you not agree with me for the usual daily wage? Take what belongs to you and go; I choose to give to this last the same as I give to you. Am I not allowed to do what I choose with what belongs to me? Or are you envious because I am generous?' So the last will be first, and the first will be last."
>
> (Matthew 20:1, 13-16 NRSV)

The landowner went out to hire workers in his field, and he hired workers throughout the day. When the working day was finished, he paid the last who arrived first. When those who worked least in the field received a full day's wage, those who had served all day were expecting to get at least time-and-a-half. When the first received the same wage as those who barely worked, they became angry and upset. The landowner responded saying, "Am I not allowed to do what I choose with what belongs to me? Or are you envious because I am generous?" That's the thing about God's grace. It is an amazing gift when it is offered to you, but when it is granted to someone you don't think deserves it, it is the toughest pill in all of creation to swallow. God's economy doesn't follow the same rules as the world. Now, you could argue that all the workers received their agreed-upon pay; therefore the payment at the end of the day is fair, but God's justice isn't about fairness. When Mary, Jesus' mother, praises God for what God accomplishes through the Messiah, she celebrates that God lifts up the lowly, scatters the proud, and sends the rich away empty (Luke 1:46-55). Of course there are verses about how God causes it to rain on the just and unjust (see Matthew 5:45), but when Jesus talks about God's relationship with us, God seems to move toward the lowly, the poor, the outcast, and the forgotten. At least, that's where God seems to hang out.

God's economy doesn't follow the same rules as the world.

If the foundation of our relationship with God is "you reap what you sow," then Jesus' parable makes little sense. Those who worked for only an hour received a much greater return for their time than those who labored all day. It almost seems foolish to say "yes" to the landowner so early in the day. But God's grace is extravagant, abundant, and it doesn't play by the rules we expect. If we are to reap what we sow, God's grace would be out of reach. It cannot be earned. It can only be the source of our response. That's the mystery of the parable. Everyone in the field receives the agreed-upon wage. The wage is not the reward; rather it is the work itself. The work in the field is our response to God's invitation. It is the work of hospitality and welcome. It is the work of lifting up the lowly and denying the self. It is the work of loving the unlovable and welcoming the stranger. The reward found within God's grace is God's selfless invitation to incorporate us into the kind of work that transforms the individual and the world. This is why Scrooge struggles—because he begins to realize that the work is not the point. A hard day's work is the means to receiving the reward of wealth, but in the kingdom of God that Jesus came to bring into the world, the work itself is the reward.

When Mary was pregnant with Jesus, she traveled to visit her cousin Elizabeth. When they met, Mary offered a great vision of what God's kingdom looks like in the world:

Mary said,

> "With all my heart I glorify the Lord!
>> In the depths of who I am I rejoice in God my savior. . . .
>> He has pulled the powerful down from their thrones
>>> and lifted up the lowly.
> He has filled the hungry with good things
>> and sent the rich away empty-handed.
> He has come to the aid of his servant Israel,
>> remembering his mercy,
>> just as he promised to our ancestors,
>>> to Abraham and to Abraham's descendants forever."
>>> (Luke 1:46-47, 52-55)

During Advent, we remember Mary's vision of God's new creation coming into the world through Christ. It is a graceful world in which the proud are scattered, the hungry are filled, the lowly are lifted, and the hopeless are offered a new life.

Which songs from your childhood have helped you remember important lessons, and what might those lessons be?

Have you memorized any Christmas carols? Which carol best helps you share the Christmas story?

Which one of Jesus' parables is most memorable for you? Why do you suppose you remember that particular story?

GOD REST YOU MERRY, GENTLEMEN OR GOD REST YOU, MERRY GENTLEMEN

"Keep Christmas in your own way, and let me keep it in mine." (Stave One)

Early on in *A Christmas Carol*, Scrooge shoos away a lone caroler who is outside singing, "God Rest You Merry, Gentlemen," just before he offers Bob Cratchit an egregious full day off for Christmas. In dismissing the caroler, Dickens cleverly foreshadows Scrooge's midnight transformative journey.

"God Rest You Merry, Gentlemen" is a hymn that details how Christ's birth was announced first to the shepherds, who were men with little means; but by the end of the hymn, the author calls all to be joined together in brotherhood and love. Just prior to leaving the counting house, Scrooge's nephew, Fred, pays him a visit. His nephew is full of joy and merriment during the Christmas season, and he cannot understand why Scrooge is so, well, like Scrooge. He declares,

"[Christmas is] a kind, forgiving, charitable, pleasant time: the only time I know of, in the long calendar of the year, when men and women seem by one consent to open their shut-up hearts freely, and to think of people below them as if they really were fellow-passengers to the grave, and not another race of creatures bound on other journeys. And therefore, uncle, though it has never put a scrap of gold or silver in my pocket, I believe that it *has* done me good, and *will* do me good; and I say, God bless it!"

(Stave One)

Scrooge's nephew embodies what the carol "God Rest You Merry, Gentlemen" is trying to say—Christmas isn't about gaining wealth and prosperity; rather the season celebrates that all are united as one body in the hope of shared kindness and charity. Scrooge isn't swayed, however, becoming increasingly bitter as the conversation continues. He dismisses his nephew, he dismisses the caroler at the keyhole, and he dismisses the carol's message itself.

But wait, maybe we are giving Scrooge a bad rap. After all, "God Rest You Merry, Gentlemen," hasn't always been interpreted as a hopeful song about the poor being filled with good things. Interestingly, the song's title has changed through the years, and as it turns out, the placement of the comma in the title is quite important. An early version of the carol, published in 1775,[4] lists the song as, "God Rest You, Merry Gentlemen," suggesting that rest is the goal of Christ's coming into the world, and it is a rest reserved for "merry gentlemen," meaning those of means who find strength in status (think Robin Hood and his band of "merry" men). When the carol was published in 1833,[5] the title was changed to "God Rest You Merry, Gentlemen," which would suggest that "being merry" is the focus of the gospel, and it is a blessing offered to someone of high status as a reminder of Christ's lowly birth. It seems that Dickens favors this later interpretation in his 1843 work, though Dickens offers no punctuation in his citing of the song at all!

Changing the comma can mean everything. It's like the T-shirt that reads, "Let's eat grandma. Let's eat, grandma. Commas save lives." Okay, so I don't think grandma's life was ever in jeopardy, but there is a story from Scripture in which the comma is a matter of life or death. The majority of the Book of Genesis, the first book in the Bible, is devoted to telling the story of Abraham's relationship with God. God called Abraham to leave his hometown and his family behind, and to go where God was calling. Abraham was faithful to God's request, and God promised him that he would be the father of a great people. When Abraham was one hundred years old, many years after Abraham began following God, Abraham and his wife, Sarah, had their son, Isaac. It seemed that God's promise was finally coming true. But not long after Isaac was born, God made a difficult and curious request of Abraham: "Take your son, your only son whom you love, Isaac, and go to the land of Moriah. Offer him up as an entirely burned offering there on one of the mountains that I will show you" (Genesis 22:2). The obedient Abraham rose early in the morning and set out with Isaac and two other servants in order to sacrifice his son according to God's command. While on the journey, Abraham and Isaac have their only recorded conversation in the Bible:

> Isaac said to his father Abraham, "Father!" And he said, "Here I am, my son." He said, "The fire and the wood are here, but where is the lamb for a burnt offering?" Abraham said, "God himself will provide the lamb for a burnt offering, my son." So the two of them walked on together.
>
> (Genesis 22:7-8 NRSV)

Here Abraham's response exemplifies the ambiguity of the story. This statement can be understood in two completely different ways. The first, "God himself will provide the lamb, my son," seems to suggest that Abraham trusted that God was not going to allow this sacrifice to take place. The other way of hearing this statement, such as "God himself will provide the lamb . . . *my son*," (NRSV) suggests that God intended all along that Isaac was born for the sole purpose of this sacrifice. In this reading it sounds like Abraham is fully expecting to sacrifice his son. What is Abraham thinking? We don't know, and I'm not sure that we are supposed to.

Dickens was wise to leave the comma out. The ambiguity of it all helps us live into the tension of the Advent season. The four weeks before Christmas many churches celebrate a time of "waiting" for Christ's coming into the world. As we've already discussed, it's a strange thing to wait for something to happen that we know has already occurred. Some things you can only do once. For example, watching a football game doesn't have the same energy or tension when you know who will win. A surprise birthday party loses its surprise if the birthday girl knows that partygoers are hiding in the living room with the lights off. A good mystery novel isn't nearly as good if you know the butler did it in the ballroom with a candlestick.

Hope often is born out of despair because it is in the darkness that the Holy Spirit sparks our holy imaginations.

Advent is different. Christians profess that Christ was born, died, and rose again. The big reveal has been made. The church doesn't wait in expectation of what God is going to do; rather we live into the tension of where the divine meets the world, knowing that God has reconciled all things through Christ (Colossians 1:19-20), but the story isn't yet finished. Consider "God Rest You Merry, Gentlemen." The words are hopeful—"God rest you merry, gentlemen, let nothing you dismay, for Christ our Savior was born upon this day; To save us all from Satan's power when we were gone astray."[6] Yet the music is composed in a minor key, giving it a somber tone. In its own way, combining hope and despair, the song reminds us that Jesus' reconciling work is still coming into fruition. Some might say that "hope" really doesn't make sense in a world of prosperity, justice, compassion, and love. Hope often is born out of despair because it is in the darkness that the Holy Spirit sparks our holy imaginations. Jesus compares the kingdom of God to things like a mustard seed, a buried treasure, and a pearl. The mustard seed must be buried, the treasure unearthed, and the pearl harvested from under the water's surface. All of these kingdom images come to fruition in the darkness.

But there's a problem. If hope can only be born out of darkness, it makes the darkness sound necessary. In the beginning, when God created the universe, God created light and separated the darkness from it (Genesis 1:4). God did not create light and dark; God created light alone. When we experience darkness today, it is often the shadows we have created by putting things in the way of God's holy presence. Saying that we need darkness in order to have hope is a question Paul specifically addresses in Romans 6:1-2: "So what are we going to say? Should we continue sinning so grace will multiply? Absolutely not! All of us died to sin. How can we still live in it?" In other words, if hope is only born out of despair, it's as if we should pray for a world in which hope is no longer necessary, and that doesn't sound like the gospel.

I like to think about hope as "possibility." Hope is the picture of all that God can accomplish. It's true that despair can heighten our senses toward God's good intention, but seeing justice accomplished, hunger satiated, and shelter sought for the homeless hones our holy imaginations of God's work even more. "Jesus looked at them carefully and said, 'It's impossible for human beings. But all things are possible for God' " (Matthew 19:26). There will never be a day when dreaming about God's goodness will pass, so there will never be a day not in need of hope. So, we wait, we dream, we fight the good fight, we sing hopeful words to a melancholy tune, and we live into the tension of Christ's work that is not yet finished.

Can you recall a story that meant one thing to you as a child, and now means something different to you many years later?

Often our faith in God invites us to make difficult decisions for all the right reasons. Can you recall a difficult decision you've recently made?

If hope is the picture of all that God can accomplish, for what do you hope?

MARLEY'S GHOST

"There's more of gravy than of grave about you, whatever you are!" (Stave One)

Scrooge takes a slow, labored walk to Jacob Marley's old home, the home in which Scrooge now resides. As he approaches the door, he drops the keys and spends a moment groping at the ground to retrieve them in the heavy, dark fog. Looking up to unlock the door, he notices that the great knocker now appears as Marley's face, looking as a "bad lobster in a dark cellar" (Stave One). After Scrooge gathers his senses, the door knocker becomes once again as it always was, though Scrooge had never before paid it much mind. As he sits alone in his bedroom, he again begins to question his senses. He looks about the room and notices the Dutch tiles ornamenting the fireplace with images of biblical stories. Dickens doesn't say how long Scrooge has been ignorant of these powerful images, but it's safe to say they hadn't had much influence on Scrooge's demeanor. It's like being in a beautiful sanctuary surrounded by stained glass windows detailing Jesus' life and not welcoming the poor and the outcast to sit beside you.

I wonder how often God is standing right beside us and we are unaware. The Book of Hebrews reminds us, "Keep loving each other like family. Don't neglect to open up your homes to guests, because by doing this some have been hosts to angels without knowing it.... Your way of life should be free from the love of money, and you should be content with what you have. After all, he has said, *I will never leave you or abandon you*" (Hebrews 13:1-2, 5). Prevenient grace, God's movement toward us, never stops and never ends; it's just that we don't see it as often as we should. Have you ever looked back on your life and said, "God was there the whole time!" It's like the theme song to the ABC television show *The Goldbergs*, which poetically says, "I don't know the future, but the past keeps getting clearer every day."[7] After seeing Marley's face at the front door, Scrooge becomes acutely aware of his surroundings. What events in your life have made you more aware of the present? Maybe it was a fender-bender that made you more aware of your car's blind spots? Maybe you have a family member with a debilitating disease, which makes you mindful of others who are suffering, or maybe a friend was arrested and jailed, opening your eyes to our Christian calling to visit those imprisoned? How could Scrooge have missed these images surrounding his bedroom? How have we been careless to notice God's presence that never lets us go and is always near—"Where can I go from your spirit? / Or where can I flee from your presence?" (Psalm 139:7 NRSV).

As Scrooge is sleeping, the servant's bells over the door chaotically chime, waking Scrooge up from his meditative slumber, and Marley's ghost appears through the door, fettered in weight-laden chains forged with his miserly wealth. Marley says that he is restless, always traveling with an "incessant torture of remorse" (Stave One). Part of Marley's punishment is the inability to find peace, and his restlessness is one we know too well during the holidays. There are seemingly countless parties, decorations, concerts, gifts to wrap, stockings to hang (or to threaten to take down depending on one's conduct), and meals to prepare. On the other hand, there is loneliness as well—memories of loved ones no longer with us, the numbing silence of an empty house, the sadness of seeing giggling children you could never have yourself. Advent is to be a time of waiting, not only to live into the tension of when the divine and creation collide, but it is the spiritual discipline of slowing down to notice God's presence in the still small voice within a violent and hurried world. "Be still, and know that I am God!" the psalmist reminds us (Psalm 46:10 NRSV), but Marley is doomed to wander in constant aimless motion, like a shopper on Christmas Eve trying to find a last-minute gift.

Marley offers Scrooge a warning echoing Father Abraham in Jesus' "Lazarus and the Rich Man" parable:

> "There was a certain rich man who clothed himself in purple and fine linen, and who feasted luxuriously every day. At his gate lay a certain poor man named Lazarus who was covered with sores. Lazarus longed to eat the crumbs that fell from the rich man's table. Instead, dogs would come and lick his sores.

> "The poor man died and was carried by angels to Abraham's side. The rich man also died and was buried. While being tormented in the place of the dead, he looked up and saw Abraham at a distance with Lazarus at his side. He shouted, 'Father Abraham, have mercy on me. Send Lazarus to dip the tip of his finger in water and cool my tongue, because I'm suffering in this flame.' But Abraham said, 'Child, remember that during your lifetime you received good things, whereas Lazarus received terrible things. Now Lazarus is being comforted and you are in great pain. Moreover, a great crevasse has been fixed between us and you. Those who wish to cross over from here to you cannot. Neither can anyone cross from there to us.'

> "The rich man said, 'Then I beg you, Father, send Lazarus to my father's house. I have five brothers. He needs to warn them so that they don't come to this place of agony.' Abraham replied, 'They have Moses and the Prophets. They must listen to them.' The rich man said, 'No, Father Abraham! But if someone from the dead goes to them, they will change their hearts and lives.' Abraham said, 'If they don't listen to Moses and the Prophets, then neither will they be persuaded if someone rises from the dead.'"

(Luke 16:19-31)

In life the rich man could not see the poor man's value as a child of God. The poor man was neither welcome at his table nor worth his time. In the afterlife the rich man still sees Lazarus as a servant whose job it is to do the rich man's bidding—"Send Lazarus to dip his finger...Send him to my father's house..." This parable is not about the afterlife or reaping what you sow or economics or the sting of guilt; rather it offers a conviction to open our eyes to the value of each and every life. The rich man's torment is his own stubbornness in holding on to the misplaced assumption that his life is more valuable than Lazarus's. This great void between Lazarus and the rich man was not wealth or status; rather the great chasm across which the rich man cannot travel is ignorance. When we fail to see that class is a human construct built around the false belief that some souls are worth more than others, the chasm that separates us from one another is indeed impossible to cross.

When we learn to accept and share that free gift of grace, we begin to understand that Christ is living with us, that we are here on earth to serve our Father and to share that grace with one another.

In a way, Marley represents the rich man in Jesus' parable, affirming that you reap what you sow, but warning Scrooge that he has been sowing the wrong kind of seed. Scrooge cannot fathom that Marley walks in restlessness, saying, "But you were always a good man of business, Jacob," to which Marley answers, "Business!...Mankind was my business. The common welfare was my business; charity, mercy, forbearance, and benevolence were, all, my business. The dealings of my trade were but a drop of water in the comprehensive ocean of my business!" (Stave One). Along with the other spirits who roam, Marley can see the plight of the poor, but can do nothing about it other than reveal it to Scrooge.

Marley's warning can be taken too far, proclaiming that if we are filled with compassion, generosity, and selflessness, we can earn a place near the bosom of Abraham. But we do not—we cannot—earn God's grace. It is a gift freely offered to us. When we learn to accept and share that free gift of grace, we begin to understand that Christ is living with us, that we are here on earth to serve our Father and to share that grace with one another, and that the only chasms that exist are the ones we create.

If Marley's ghost were to visit you, what do you think he might say to you?

During this holiday season, how might you practice the spiritual discipline of slowing down to notice God's presence?

How do you feel called to respond to God's grace?

You Cannot Serve Two Masters

*"Why did I walk through crowds of fellow-beings with my
eyes turned down, and never raise them to that blessed Star
which led the Wise Men to a poor abode! Were there no
poor homes to which its light would have conducted me!"*
- Marley to Scrooge (Stave One)

Before Marley's spirit disappears, he leads Scrooge to the window to see a plethora of ghosts moaning and crying out (wailing and gnashing their teeth, perhaps?) in sorrow and in torment. Dickens writes, "The misery with them all was, clearly, that they sought to interfere, for good, in human matters, and had lost the power for ever" (Stave One). Scrooge begins to say "Humbug!" to them all, but he can only mutter a monosyllabic "Hum…," signaling a glimmer of change within his soul. These spirits' punishment is being able to see great need in the world, and no longer having the ability to intervene. It's as though, for example, they are full of love but unable to share it. They can never satisfy their hunger to love their neighbor as themselves. At this point in the story, Scrooge is filled only with a love of money, and it's as if Marley is trying to warn him that ultimately, in the end, money will not fill the void Scrooge will feel when it's all he has left.

Money is a funny thing, isn't it? At times it can be empowering, helping you do things you never thought possible, and other times it makes you feel worthless, as though you can contribute nothing to the world. Some say it makes the world go round; others say the love of it is the root of all evil. Whether it's made of nickel or paper or it's torn from a book or is a digital bitcoin, money is simply a means of making change. For example, if I have a cow and you have a chicken, and I need a chicken and you need a cow, then we might have a quick and easy trade. Except, is a cow worth what a chicken is worth? If not, then someone is getting a bad deal. I can't cut a deal with you because I literally don't want to cut up my cow. Money simply is the means of making change so that we can trade cows and chickens more fairly.

For me, money has held different value at different times in my life. In junior high school, I understood money in terms of compact discs. If I cut the grass, I could buy two albums at the store. In high school, it meant tanks of gas. In undergrad, it was measured in cases of beer. In graduate school, it was pounds of coffee. As a parent, it is in packs of diapers. Money is worth what our culture says it is worth. This system works fine until there is a dramatic cultural shift, such as during the subprime housing market shift in 2007 or the downturn of the Louisiana oil industry in 1985 or the bust of

America's economy in 1929 and so on. When there is a dramatic shift in the culture, what the culture values can also shift.

In the Book of Exodus, Pharaoh sent word to Moses saying, "Take your people and leave." So the people got up quickly, not waiting for their bread to rise, though they did spend some time plundering the Egyptians on their way out, and they set out to cross the Red Sea into the wilderness to escape from Pharaoh's mighty oppression (Exodus 12:33-36). They were filled with great devotion to God, who had loosened the bonds of slavery. One of the ways the ancient Israelites offered devotion to God was through burnt offerings, burning the meat and fat of livestock. Burning this meat and fat meant that it could not be used for food or material wealth, so it was quite a sacrifice for the people (and certainly the animal itself) to burn away such a precious commodity. Scripture says that the people followed God through the wilderness via a pillar of cloud by day and pillar of fire by night. This seems like a strange and supernatural experience, but this makes beautiful sense because the burning of their offerings on the altar appeared like a pillar of cloud during the day and a pillar of fire by night. In other words, their sacrifices to God, their devotion to the Lord, led the way through the wilderness (Exodus 13:21).

Even though their devotion to God was ever before them, it wasn't long before they were hungry and there was no food and they were thirsty and there was nothing to drink. The ancient Israelites experienced a radical new reality, and so their values changed. They started looking over their shoulders, grumbling, "At least under slavery in Egypt we had food and water. We would rather die in Egypt than die out here" (see Exodus 16:3). The riches they had plundered from the Egyptians had no value in the middle of the desert. Moses said the Lord would make it rain bread from heaven. Early in the morning when the dew had burned away, the ancient Israelites saw white, flaky stuff on the ground and said, "Manna," which means, "What is this?" God had blessed them with "whatever" it was to get them through the day. Moses told the people to gather only the manna they needed, nothing more. Some gathered plenty, and others gathered little; but for those who gathered more than what they needed, the abundance spoiled.

I've heard hell described as a place in which one can have too much and not enough at the same time, that in hell you can have anything you can dream up. So, if I want a one-hundred-inch big-screen TV, I can have it. The problem is, the guy living next to me can have my TV too should he wish it. I would imagine that eventually quarreling becomes so terrible that humanity becomes increasingly isolated. Stuff becomes our master. This hell is a place in which we can have anything we want, but the stuff we want leaves us lonely, isolated, and depressed.

So how do I know if I have enough? The author of Proverbs 30 offers interesting reflection—"Fraud and lies— / keep far from me! / Don't give me either poverty or wealth; / give me just the food I need. / Or I'll be full and deny you, / and say, 'Who is the LORD?' / Or I'll be poor and steal, / and dishonor my God's name." (Proverbs 30:8-9). In other words, this author is crying out for enough. He doesn't want too much because he knows that having great wealth tempts us into idolatry and undermines our reliance on God. Likewise, being caught in the cycle of abject poverty can lead one to a cynical place where mention of God's goodness seems unattainable.

He begins by asking for God to keep fraud and lies far from him. In other words, whether we have too much or whether we are in want, the point is to reflect truth: the truth that God makes it rain on the just and unjust, the truth that you cannot serve both God and money, the truth that valuing profit over people is far from God's heart, the truth that the master invited the poor, the blind, and the lame to the table because the elite were too busy (Luke 14:21), the truth that Christ's resurrection changed the rules of the world and we are no longer slaves to the mammon of human hands.

In Matthew 6, Jesus says that you cannot serve two masters. You will either love the first and hate the second or hate the first and love the second. You cannot serve both God and mammon or wealth (Matthew 6:24, also Luke 16:13). Another way to frame it is, "You cannot serve Manna and Mammon." One Saturday morning, the church where I serve offered the community a "free" garage sale. Folks came and began browsing and we all shared the normal Saturday morning garage sale conversation ("How are you?" ... "The weather's beautiful today" ... "I'm watching the game later" ...), and then we would hand them a card with church information and say, "By the way, everything is already paid for." Most people stopped and looked back with unbelief.

"You mean it's free?"

"Yes, take what you need."

It's almost if they could not imagine the concept. You could see the confused, but joyful, look on their faces as they gathered what they needed without having to offer anything in return. The truth is we cannot serve both God and money, and the first step toward that truth is opening up our holy imagination to a world in which money is not in charge. Hear me when I say that, yes, money is necessary in our world. Money is a means of making change, and when our imagination is open to the Holy Spirit, change can actually happen.

The truth is we cannot serve both God and money, and the first step toward that truth is opening up our holy imagination to a world in which money is not in charge.

But Scrooge's *only* love is money, and Marley warns him that this misplaced love will become nothing more than heavy chains in the afterlife. In a way, these chains are like the ancient Israelites' life of slavery in Egypt—it wasn't great, but it was what they had accepted as their life. Scrooge had to let go of Egypt, that familiar, comfortable place of slavery to work and money, so that his hands could be open to the manna that only God could provide, a sustenance that is exactly what we need. It is the grace of God that meets us in the wilderness, the bounty that is offered in sacrifice and shared with each other. It is the pillar of cloud and fire leading the way to the heart of God.

What are some ways you offer devotion to God? Do you tithe? Do you serve at your church and community? What gift do you offer to God?

Of what is God calling you to "let go" so that you might be free to live out your commitment to Christ?

What would you consider to be modern-day manna? What is something God freely offers to you?

Reflection: A New View

"Bah!... Humbug!... Merry Christmas! What right have you to be merry?... What's Christmas time to you but a time for paying bills without money; a time for finding yourself a year older, but not an hour richer?" (Stave One)

Jesus turned to the woman and said to Simon, "Do you see this woman? When I entered your home, you didn't give me water for my feet, but she wet my feet with tears and wiped them with her hair." (Luke 7:44)

Do you know any Scrooges around your Christmas tree or in your church pew? It's easy to dismiss them or conveniently forget to mail their invitations to the ugly sweater contest. A curmudgeon can quickly ruin a party or make things awkward during the gift exchange. Many of us might react to Scrooge the way Bob Cratchit's wife did: "I wish I had him here. I'd give him a piece of my mind to feast upon, and I hope he'd have a good appetite for it" (Stave Three).

You probably would have called my friend Stacy a Scrooge. Several years ago, I noticed that Christmas was not a happy time for her. Stacy wouldn't sing the Christmas carols on Sunday, and she would apathetically sit in worship, unmoved even when the children dressed up in period costumes, fumbled to recite Scripture, and pulled a wooden donkey to a makeshift manger.

One Sunday after worship I asked Stacy why she seemed to be so down at Christmas time. At first she shrugged and said, "This just isn't a happy time for me," then walked away. Later that week, she came back and told me her father had died many years ago on Christmas morning, and all the happiness, cheer, and glad tidings had drained from the holiday. Each year, experiencing Christmas again felt like reopening a wound she desperately wanted to heal.

One of the things I love about Dickens's story is that we receive an intimate glimpse into Scrooge and discover why he is the way he is. Every Scrooge in our own lives has a story. Usually, though, we aren't able to hear that story unless the person trusts us enough to share it, as Stacy did.

After hearing her story, I invited Stacy to our staff Christmas gathering, and she was thankful to celebrate the season with her church family. The following Christmas, I noticed a small change in the way she sat in the pew. When we sang "Silent Night, Holy Night" I looked at Stacy's face and saw tears instead of indifference. For those who struggle with depression, tears can be a hopeful sign.

Next time you run across a Scrooge at Christmas, maybe you can view "Bah! Humbug!" in a new way. When Simon objected to the woman who washed Jesus' feet with her tears, Jesus asked him, "Do you see this woman?" (Luke 7:44).

Maybe the first step toward a merry Christmas is to look at those who are suffering and, quite simply, to see.

Gracious God, give us eyes to see the unhappy and the misunderstood, and the ears to hear their story. Help us to share Christ through humble invitation, especially with those who are in need of healing. May Christ's welcoming Spirit live within us. Amen.

CHAPTER TWO

THE REMEMBRANCE OF CHRISTMAS PAST

*"Bear but a touch of my hand there," said the Spirit,
laying it upon his heart, "and you shall be upheld in more
than this!" (Stave Two)*

"The past" is quite a small phrase for something representing everything that has happened up until your reading of this word. Sometimes we qualify the word *past* with adjectives like *recent* or *distant* or *forgotten*, but even then it's hard to know how *distant* distant is supposed to be. One week before Christmas 2015, the New Orleans City Council approved the removal of Confederate monuments from public landmarks by a six-to-one margin. The most heated debate was over whether the city should remove the General Robert E. Lee statue from Lee Circle, a very popular landmark

49

on St. Charles Avenue. This debate is probably quite similar to disagreements happening wherever you might live about how we should honor, remember, and move on from our past. In this debate, there is certainly room to discuss and debate the meaning of art. Artwork such as statues, emblems, and symbols are powerful vehicles through which we discover and share our identity as a culture. But what complicates these discussions is that the meaning behind this art is almost completely subjective. Who has the authority to say what a symbol means? When sharing matters of opinion, I usually find it best to listen rather than argue why my opinion is more holy or informed than someone else's. Everyone is entitled to her or his own opinion; however no one is entitled to his or her own facts.

One of the things I heard during the debate was, "You can't change Lee Circle. It's always been Lee Circle." In actuality, until 1884 it was known as Tivoli Circle. It's true that no one alive today was around to enjoy Tivoli Circle, but to assume that my experiences during my lifetime is the way things always have been or the way things always should be is wrong. We should certainly remember our past, but how far back should we go? Is 1884 far enough? If so, then the statue becomes meaningless without remembering the Civil War of the 1860s itself. Scrooge comes face to face with the Ghost of Christmas Past, and in doing so, he is reminded of things that have happened to him in the past. These remembrances bring him both joy and pain, but they help remind him of who he was and from where he came.

WISE MEN AT THE NATIVITY

"The voice was soft and gentle. Singularly low, as if instead of being so close beside him, it were at a distance."

(Stave Two)

ADVENT WEEK 2: HOPE

The week of Advent we light the candle of Hope. Hebrews 11:1 says, "Faith is the reality of what we hope for, the proof of what we don't see." Hope is the destination of our faith. It is not enough to be faithful, trusting in what your eyes do not see. I might believe I can fly, but leaping from a tall building without a parachute is still a bad idea. I might believe that my candidate will win the election, but if my candidate's faithful voters do not turn up at the polls, a victory will not be possible. A hopeless faith is like getting in the car for a weekend trip, not knowing where you are going. You trust that the trip will go well and that you will return safely, but without a destination, you will wander aimlessly. Hope is what keeps us from following a blind faith. Hope is the destination.

Before lighting the candles of Love and Joy, we must begin with Hope. The Old Testament offers prophetic words of a time when God will rescue God's people. In Isaiah we find, "The people who walked in darkness / have seen a great light; / those who lived in a land of deep darkness— / on them light has shined.... / For a child has been born for us, / a son given to us; / authority rests upon his shoulders" (Isaiah 9:2, 6 NRSV). These and many other Old Testament teachings guide our faith during the Advent season for a time in which God will reconcile all things (Colossians 1:20). Our hope is reconciliation, forgiveness, grace, and salvation, and that hope grounds our faith.

Gracious God, ground our faith in the hope of salvation. Let us not walk aimlessly in darkness, but let us see the light that Christ will bring into the world. In the name of the Father and of the Son and of the Holy Spirit. Amen.

I love the way Dickens describes the voice of the Ghost of Christmas Past: "The voice was soft and gentle. Singularly low, as if instead of being so close beside him, it were at a distance" (Stave Two). I think this perfectly describes memories—sometimes it seems as if our memories are right next to us but also "at a distance."

What is your earliest memory? When you close your eyes and attempt to recall it, does your mind jump from image to image like a poorly edited movie? Maybe what you see is vivid and definitive. Perhaps it feels like a singular perspective that no one else will ever know or see. In my earliest memory, I see a scene in which my little sister is running away from me down the sidewalk during a game of tag. The interesting thing about this memory being my earliest is that I have no recollection of ever being an only child. Even though I was on the scene three years before my sister, I have always seen myself as a brother (to two sisters, in fact). That's the funny thing about memories. They feel true and intimate, they help shape our identities and how we see the world, but sometimes our memories are incomplete, blindly subjective, and even misleading. This can be especially true of our distant memories, in which we assume that our experiences were the way things were *supposed* to be, to the point where we can find ourselves replicating our missteps and faults from the past.

What do you "remember" about the Christmas story? Of course you weren't there, but if you had to write out the highlights of the first Nativity, what would you include? How about this version: *Joseph and Mary were engaged to be married, but before they were married, Mary became pregnant by the Holy Spirit. Joseph wanted to dismiss her but was told in a dream not to. Mary had the baby, and the baby was called Jesus.* This version seems frightfully unimpressive to me. For example, where are the angels? What about "no room in the inn"? Where are the shepherds? What about the wise men who traversed afar? Actually, these few lines are, more or less, what Matthew actually reports about Jesus' birth in Matthew 1:18-25. Actually, what we recall of the Christmas story in the Bible is a combination of Matthew's Gospel and Luke's Gospel. We tend to combine the two, including everything we can in one, neat narrative, even going so far as to having the wise men show up in the Nativity scene. (They weren't there, but I'd challenge you to find me a Nativity set that doesn't include these guys with their gifts of gold, frankincense, and myrrh.)

Now there's nothing *wrong* with having a star, a manger, and wise men all in the same place, but what this helps us to realize is that sometimes our memory of how we think things are *supposed* to be might not be the best picture of what they *should* be. We can get very frustrated when our picture of what Christmas should be doesn't measure up. "Keep Christmas in your own way, and let me keep it in mine," Scrooge says to his nephew in the counting house (Stave One).

I have fond memories of coming home from the Christmas Eve candlelight service and opening presents with the family after a delicious and filling dinner. For me, going to church, having dinner, opening presents, and getting to bed early was what Christmas was all about. I remember the first Christmas my wife and I shared after we were married. We sang the old hymns arm in arm, we lit each other's "Silent Night" candles, and we held hands while walking to the car in the muggy South Louisiana weather. It was as perfect as anyone might hope. After getting into the car, I leaned over and gave her a kiss, saying how thankful I was for where we were. I told her that I loved sharing Christmas Eve with her. As we drove away I said, "I am so excited to go home and open presents with you," to which she replied, "We don't open presents on Christmas Eve. You're supposed to wait until Christmas morning." I hit the brakes harder than I would like to admit, and I looked at her with a "Who are you and what kind of madness did you just say?" kind of expression. You know those things about marriage that no one tells you about but you just have to figure out on your own? This was one of them. Of course at the time I wasn't smart enough to quickly say, "You didn't let me finish. I can't wait to go home and open presents with you...in the morning."

In a small way, my picture of a traditional Christmas had changed. Have you ever had an experience that dramatically changed what Christmas looks like to you? Maybe Christmas was a happy time until a close family member or friend died. Maybe your Christmases were difficult until that one year when someone gave you a gift that changed everything. Maybe you're still waiting to figure out what Christmas is all about. For good or ill, our memories shape who we are, and these memories offer us a default picture of what the world is and our role within it.

Scrooge seems to have forgotten his own story. He is always bitter and exasperated at the people around him, but as the story unfolds we find out this wasn't always the case. The Ghost of Christmas Past takes Scrooge on a journey to his hometown, and immediately he was filled with joy. His lip quivers, and a single tear falls upon his cheek. Do you have memories that overwhelm you, like that holy moment when you unwrap a forgotten ornament given to you by someone special? There is a small but interesting detail in *Carol* when Scrooge first sees his hometown. Scrooge sees young boys in great spirits enjoying the crisp Christmas air. You get the sense that Scrooge calls out to them to somehow share in their excitement, although Dickens doesn't mention Scrooge's reaction. " 'These are but shadows of the things that have been,' said the Ghost. 'They have no consciousness of us' " (Stave Two). Scrooge, who is very real, cannot interact with the joy he sees from his projected memory, in much the same way the souls who roam the earth are unable to give aid to the very real suffering of the destitute in the dark streets of London. Although this hometown scene is a jolly one, Scrooge is unable to interact with his surroundings and share in this joy. Like the rich man who is separated from Lazarus by a great chasm, Scrooge can see glad tidings happening around him, but he just cannot connect with them.

Christ died and was raised, not to prevent us from grieving, but so that our brokenness would be redeemed, our faults would not define us, and our sadness would not be the end of the story.

Recently my church hosted a Christmas healing service where we invited those for whom the holiday season is difficult to join us for prayer, meditation, and Holy Communion. During our time of sharing, it was hard not to openly weep from the stories we heard. One woman talked about how her father had died on Christmas morning. Another cried out, "I wish my son could forgive me." Another remembered how lonely he was now that his wife was gone. It was a beautiful lament. We shared in each other's grief. When I broke the bread around the Communion table, I mentioned how our salvation is brought about not through wholeness, but through a broken body. Christ died and was raised, not to prevent us from grieving, but so that our brokenness would be redeemed, our faults would not define us, and our sadness would not be the end of the story. The next morning, the woman who wept over her father's death called me to say that she had a profound sense of peace during the service. It's not that her sadness was gone, but when we shared the bread and the cup she felt that she had gained permission to once again be happy during Christmas. She felt that her sadness was a means of remembering and honoring her father. In other words, being happy during Christmas felt offensive to her memory. But knowing that brokenness can be redeemed offered her a holy moment of forgiving herself. Could it be that Scrooge's inability to be merry was a way of honoring his heartbreak, ensuring that the pain he remembered was not dismissed or understood as unimportant? It seems that the gospel teaches us that we honor our pain, not by holding on to it, but by sharing it and carrying it with each other. In other words, Christ died and rose again. Christ was laid in the tomb, but that is not where he stayed. Suffering is certainly part of the story, but it is neither where the story lingers nor ends.

Our memories are not always accurate. Sometimes our visions of the past are incomplete or misleading, emphasizing sadness while forgetting joy. When we gather for worship around the Communion table we are called to remember Christ—"Do this in remembrance of me" (Luke 22:19). Jesus knows our faults and our faulty memories and yet invites us to the table anyway. Daily connecting with Christ doesn't mean we will be perfect and always filled with happiness, but it does mean through Christ we will remember that we have been redeemed and will be transformed to accept and share love with God and our neighbor. I've heard love described as someone who knows you well and loves you anyway, and Christ indeed loves us.

Do you have a Nativity scene in your home? What story does it tell? If I didn't know the scriptural account of Jesus' birth, what would I learn just from seeing your Nativity scene?

What do you consider to be the most important elements of the Christmas season? How do you feel when those elements are missing from your celebration? Which elements help you remember Christ during the season?

A GLIMPSE OF REDEMPTION

"There was a boy singing a Christmas Carol at my door last night. I should like to have given him something: that's all." (Stave Two)

I remember when I first discovered that my parents weren't perfect. As a child my dad was basically a superhero. He had the answer to every homework question, he always came home at about the same time, he sang in the church choir, and he could identify constellations in the sky. Every Wednesday evening, our family would go out to dinner. It was weekly check-in with each other, and it was one of my favorite things. We were always involved in church activities, after-school sports, and music ensembles, so having at least one meal together was an important family tradition. One Wednesday afternoon when I was in the seventh grade, I saw my dad's car pull into the driveway, and I ran out to meet him. I greeted him as his car door opened and asked, "Where are we eating tonight, Dad?" He was slumped, clutching his left arm. He walked quickly past me. "Nowhere!" he said. I froze. I didn't know what was happening. My mother walked us over to the neighbor's home before she took my father to the hospital. A day later we heard that he'd had a heart attack.

When I finally made it to the hospital, I saw my dad connected to machines and a great sadness filled me. I wasn't really crying for my dad; rather I was broken because, for the first time in my life, Superman was vulnerable. In a way, I had been viewing my father from a distance, but his heart attack quickly transported me close enough to see the cracks in the tile. The next few months were difficult. Because my dad was recovering at home, my sisters and I had to miss ballet and baseball practice, sleepovers and parties. I remember him sitting with us in the living room, and in a moment of vulnerable honesty, he apologized for making us miss so much. It was the first time I saw my father cry. Instead of feeling angry for missing out, I realized my profound love for my dad.

When Scrooge sees his former self he realizes, maybe for the first time, how utterly lonely he was as a child. His friends failed to include him for sleigh rides, his family was so distant they aren't included in his Christmas-past vision, and his own imagination was his only companion. Instead of being filled with blame or anger against those who created his loneliness, he is moved to compassion. When the spirit notices his emotion he asks what is the matter. Scrooge replies, "Nothing. There was a boy singing a Christmas Carol at my door last night. I should like to have given him something: that's all" (Stave Two). Instead of offering a dismissive "Humbug," or angry soliloquy, he laments missing an opportunity to make a difference for another. Instead of anger over his tragic childhood, he is convicted toward ensuring that others will have a different experience. In other words, Scrooge is beginning to build an intimate relationship with himself, or at least the person he used to be before he lost himself in his pursuit of wealth.

What do you see when you look in the mirror? Do you see yourself as a child of God? It can be difficult to look in the mirror and know the person looking back isn't perfect. The good news is that perfection isn't a prerequisite. Following Jesus is not about never messing up, but about how, through grace, we accept our imperfections and transform them into good works. One day as Jesus walked along the Sea of Galilee, he called out to Peter, Andrew, James, and John saying, "Drop your nets and follow me" (see Matthew 4:19). So they dropped their nets and followed. Well, that was an awfully short sermon. I imagine that if Jesus asked Peter, Andrew, James, and John the ordination examination questions in the United Methodist *Book of Discipline*, things wouldn't have gone so well.

"Do you trust that you are called by God to the life and work of a pastor?"

"Uh, well, I don't know. I was fishing just a few moments ago."

"Do you believe in the Triune God?"

"I'm not sure. What does *Triune* mean?"

"Are you persuaded that the Old and New Testaments—"

"Sorry to interrupt, but what's a New Testament?"

Jesus must have had amazing charisma for fishermen to drop their day jobs and immediately follow him. Maybe the secret is a one-sentence sermon, though I would imagine that even the most faithful person would be hesitant in following a stranger who only had one sermon. So maybe the miracle isn't what the disciples saw in Jesus; rather the miracle is what Jesus saw in them. Paul says, "We live by faith and not by sight" (2 Corinthians 5:7). In other words, Jesus did not see them for who they were, but who they were called to become. Jesus did not see them as fishermen, but fishers of men, fishers of people. Jesus saw them not for what they had done, but for what they would do for God's kingdom. Christ doesn't call us to follow because we are perfect, but because through Christ we are perfected in love. That's one of the tenets of the United Methodist tradition, that in this lifetime the Holy Spirit will perfect us in love. This doesn't mean that we will make perfect decisions or that we are infallible or that we never screw up. "Christian perfection" is about having a perfect love of God. To put it another way, we are called to love God and neighbor by following God's perfect plan for our lives. This doesn't mean that we have to be perfect ourselves—because we won't be.

Christ doesn't call us to follow because we are perfect, but because through Christ we are perfected in love.

There is a hilarious sketch from the British comedy program *Monty Python's Flying Circus* about a confused tourist who sees that a local shepherd's sheep have decided to climb trees in order to fly. The tourist asks why the sheep are in the trees, and the shepherd replies, "It's my belief that these sheep are laboring under the misapprehension that they're birds. . . . Notice that they do not so much fly as plummet. . . . Talk about the blind leading the blind."[1] A sheep cannot live its calling if it's trying to be a bird. Nor can we live out what God is calling us to if we are climbing up the wrong trees. Sometimes we think of perfection as having no faults; but perfection, in terms of our walk with Christ, is following in the way Christ is calling us to follow. Some are called to follow Christ in the way they teach children, or respond to emergencies, or lead a company, or organize a soup kitchen, or as Paul says, "Now there are varieties of gifts, but the same Spirit...strive for the greater gifts. And I will show you a still more excellent way" (1 Corinthians 12:4, 31 NRSV).

We are not called to be perfect so much as we are perfectly suited with a gift through which we respond to God's grace. Scrooge is beginning to realize how the person he is doesn't look much like the person he once was. His bitterness has consumed any hint of love or joy he once knew. In a way, he's been walking down a path not intended for him to tread—he is not living the perfect plan for his life. I am not perfect, and neither are you, but we are perfectly made to follow Christ.

What do you think is your spiritual gift? What do you think is not?

Why do you think reflecting on his past caused Scrooge to move toward compassion rather than anger?

Flying sheep may be a silly example, but have you ever felt really out of place? How did you make a change? Who helped you find your place?

A SEASON OF SENSES: SIGHT AND TASTE

He was conscious of a thousand odours floating in the air, each one connected with a thousand thoughts, and hopes, and joys, and cares long, long, forgotten! (Stave Two)

Christmas is a season for the senses. When Scrooge sees his hometown, he is "conscious of a thousand odours floating in the air, each one connected with a thousand thoughts, and hopes, and joys, and cares long, long, forgotten!" (Stave Two). Sights and smells immediately flood his memory. At what point in the season does it "feel" like Christmas for you? Is it when the radio stations change to a Christmas song lineup? Maybe it's when the neighbors hang lights from the rooftop? Maybe it isn't Christmas until your grandmother gifts you with an unwanted fruitcake still in last year's packaging? Could it be that Jesus isn't ready to be born until spruce-scented candles are stocked at the end of the grocer's aisles?

Unlike any other time of year (with the exception of maybe Mardi Gras in New Orleans), during the Christmas season it seems as though everything changes—popular music includes sleigh bells, coffee shops offer gingerbread lattes, manger scenes adorn frosted lawns, and everything smells like pine, cranberries, and shortbread cookies. I believe that the dramatic and pervasive seasonal change is the world begging for the church to make sense of it all. It's like when you fall in love. When you find someone who makes your heart beat a little faster, the smile on your face remains a little longer, and your thoughts drift into a future you didn't think possible. You notice that everything seems different, and you wonder why you'd never seen the world like this before. Because love changes everything.

Everything changed when God put on flesh and was born in Bethlehem. God so loved the world that God became part of it so that everything within might be transformed. The changes we experience during the Advent and Christmas season are the expressions of a subconscious memory. When Jesus entered the world, everything changed, and whether we are aware, saint and sinner alike can't help but change our lights, sounds, tastes, touch, and smells in order to make sense of it all. Christmas is a season of senses through which the world is begging for meaning.

The first change I notice around Christmastime has to do with the sense of sight. The days become shorter, so we decorate our homes and businesses with lights. We seem to have a deep-seated desire to dispel the darkness, as if with each string of lights we hang, our fear of darkness diminishes. Before Scrooge journeys with the first ghost, Dickens's story is both figuratively and literally dark. We first see Scrooge in his counting house against the "cold, bleak, biting weather" (Stave One) with only a single coal in Cratchit's fireplace to light the way. Cleverly, the Ghost of Christmas Past brings Scrooge to his hometown in the light of day. Our first glimpse of a joyful Scrooge is also *Carol's* first setting in the sunlight. The Gospel of John reminds us that Christ is the light of the world—"All things came into being through him, and without him not one thing came into being. What has come into being in him was life, and the life was the light of all people. The light shines in the darkness, and the darkness did not overcome it" (John 1:3-5 NRSV). The same holds true near the end of John's Gospel during the Resurrection account—"Early on the first day of the week, while it was still dark, Mary Magdalene came to the tomb and saw that the stone had been removed from the tomb" (John 20:1 NRSV). Indeed, the darkness could not overcome the light within Christ!

Not only do we begin to announce the changing season with light, but we also try to make sense of change through decorative symbols. Those abandoned parking lots near the center of town are now packed with Christmas trees for sale. Evergreen wreaths ornamented with red berries are hung on doorways and streetlamps. Shop windows are frosted, snowmen appear on lawns over the weekend, and stop-motion television specials about Santa Claus dominate the evening schedule. One of my favorite Christmas ornaments is of Scrooge carrying Tiny Tim on his shoulder. I think of this ornament because it reminds me that Scrooge's story is one that ends well. Symbols such as these are important and effective ways to share our faith. Each year in my church we celebrate a "Hanging of the Greens" service in which we invite the youth in our congregation to share the meaning of Christmas symbols in the sanctuary. We light the Advent wreath to remember that Christ is the light of the world. We adorn the Communion rail with evergreen garlands to symbolize our faith in everlasting life. We ornament a tree with symbols from our faith as we teach children the meaning behind the dove, the Trinity, the cross, and the Bethlehem star. All of these visuals help us remember and share God's story and find our role within it. When Jesus read from the scroll of Isaiah in Luke's Gospel, he said, "The Spirit of the Lord is upon me because he has anointed me to bring…recovery of sight to the blind" (Luke 4:18 NRSV). In a way, when we fill the night with lights, our doorways with wreaths, and our trees with symbols from our faith, we carry on Jesus' mission of offering the world a new vision.

I will not apologize that another of my favorite signals that Christmas is near appeals to my sense of taste. Each year I can almost taste the anticipation when the local coffee shop introduces the annual gingerbread latte. Even though technology allows us to enjoy lots of foods outside of their normal seasons (peaches in the winter, grapes in the spring, cranberries in the summer), there's something blessed about that first taste of a seasonal dish. During the Advent season, the church talks a lot about anticipation and the eager waiting for Jesus' arrival. Sometimes this is a hopeful anticipation—such as seeing a small box under the tree and knowing that your hints at the jewelry store have paid off—but often waiting is an agonizing experience because when we wait, when we slow down, our souls suddenly become vulnerable.

I don't know about your household, but growing up my household was a zoo. When I would come home from school, mom would be doing laundry while stirring dinner and my sister would be practicing the piano while practicing ballet. My other sister would be watching TV and listening to the radio while doing homework. I would go and play video games while practicing voice lessons while daydreaming. Dad was the calm one in our house, but he was mostly at work. I don't know about your household, but I'm guessing you can identify with the craziness. I wonder if we fill up our schedules each and every day, not because there are things we have to do, but maybe we are filling our schedules simply for the sake of being busy. Because when we're not busy, brothers and sisters have to play with one another, husbands and wives have to talk with each other, families have to sit around a table and talk about their day. See, when we have to wait, when we have to slow down, when the distractions are gone, we are forced to be vulnerable.

We celebrate Advent every year so that we can mold and shape the desire we have for the presents under the tree into a desire for the Christ who was placed upon the tree.

When we slow down, when we become vulnerable by waiting, we are making room in our souls for desire. This is what happens when a child sits in front of the presents under the tree, staring, dreaming of what lies under the red-and-green paper. It may seem like the child is wasting time, but that doesn't mean there's not an important lesson to be learned in that moment. By sitting there, wasting time, and slowing down, the child is making room for desire, allowing the excitement and wonder and imagination to settle into the child's being. The beautiful thing about Advent is that it gives us permission to do the same thing—to slow down, to waste time, to allow room in our souls for desire; to sit and waste time with an old friend, to again feel the desire of friendship; to sit and waste time with your spouse, to again feel the desire within marriage; to sit and waste time with your siblings, to feel the desire of family; to sit in the sanctuary, staring at the Advent wreath, getting lost in the Christmas tree, kneeling at the table, in order to be filled with the desire to see the radiant beams of the Christ Child's holy face.

We celebrate Advent every year so that we can mold and shape the desire we have for the presents under the tree into a desire for the Christ who was placed upon the tree. We waste time so that we may immerse ourselves in the bittersweetness of the vulnerable "taste" of anticipation. This waiting tempers our souls so that we might slow down enough to see God's blessings around us, to hear the cry of those in need, to reach out our hands to embrace those in need of love, and to hunger and thirst for justice and kindness. During Christmas everything changes, and God invites us to slow down so that we might notice the change happening within our own souls.

Some people feel that reliving the past is a "waste of time," but how does doing just that have a profound effect on Scrooge's perspective?

Is your Christmas season filled with anticipation, patient waiting, or exhaustion? Why do you think it's that way?

What do you anticipate God accomplishing this year during Advent/ Christmas?

A Season of Senses: Sound and Touch

In came a fiddler with a music-book, and went up to the lofty desk, and made an orchestra of it, and tuned like fifty stomach-aches. (Stave Two)

To say I have a great eye for decorating or a refined palate for the finer foods would be a lie, but I do pride myself on my taste in music, especially Christmas music. I appreciate the holiness of hymns like "Lo, How a Rose E'er Blooming," and the haunting minor key of "What Child Is This." I love singing "Angels We Have Heard on High," while watching children sing "Glo-ooooo-ooooo-ooooo-ria" with reckless abandon. And you just can't beat singing "Silent Night, Holy Night" by candlelight at the close of a midnight mass. Of course there are the guilty pleasures of "Step Into Christmas" by Elton John, "Last Christmas" by Wham!, and the timeless "All I Want for Christmas" by Mariah Carey.

I'm not sure I can imagine what Christmas would be like without music, but interestingly, music isn't mentioned in the Christmas story at all. We often assume that when the angels appeared before the shepherds they sang, "Glory to God in heaven," but I was sad the day I realized the story simply says that they were "praising" (see Luke 2:13), which doesn't necessarily mean they were singing. As a former vocal music major, I feel that music is somehow fundamental to our existence. When God created the heavens and the earth, God created through sound. God spoke everything into existence. I wonder what the first few days of creation sounded like? Was light a simple melody? Did the separation of the waters bring forth harmony? It's no surprise to me that we have interpreted Christmas as a time that demands music. It is almost as if the songs we've created are an attempt to tap into the first sounds of the new creation set about through Jesus.

One of Scrooge's fondest memories centers around music. In his youth, Scrooge was an apprentice for a gentleman named Mr. Fezziwig. One Christmas Eve there was a grand party filled with music, dancing, and an outstanding banquet. Scrooge remembered seeing Mr. and Mrs. Fezziwig dance, recalling:

> A positive light appeared to issue from Fezziwig's calves. They shone in every part of the dance like moons. You couldn't have predicted, at any given time, what would become of them next.

And when old Fezziwig and Mrs. Fezziwig had gone all through the dance; advance and retire, both hands to your partner, bow and curtsey, corkscrew, thread-the-needle, and back again to your place; Fezziwig "cut"—cut so deftly, that he appeared to wink with his legs, and came upon his feet again without a stagger.

(Stave Two)

Music and dancing is what I envision when thinking about the moment when God created the heavens and the earth. Music is one of God's greatest gifts, and like most blessings, it is both simple and complex. At its simplest explanation, music is simply vibration moving through the air, but how powerful it is! Music has the power to create a smile and bring forth tears. Music pumps us up for the big game and soothes the angry child. It allows us to express passion, frustration, love, and beauty when words fall short. God could have created through lightning or cloud or fire, but God spoke, allowing words to travel through the chaos. It is no surprise to me that God spoke creation into existence because music invites movement. God speaks, "Let there be," and light bursts forth, dispelling the darkness. "Let there be," and waters separate, such as when royalty enters the ballroom. "Let there be," and mountains stand tall, trying their best to reach the heavens. "Let there be," and the space is filled with life. Music moves us emotionally, helping us share sadness, joy, excitement, and pain. Music calls us to clap our hands and dance to the beat. Music stretches our minds to appreciate the relationship between time and pitch and tenor. Music moves our soul, mind, and body into communion with the God who spoke life into existence.

Remembering Mr. and Mrs. Fezziwig twirling around brings Scrooge joy because music and dance call us to remember the beginning when there was no room for darkness, sadness, pain, or grief. In this moment of remembering, Scrooge is filled with such delight that he momentarily forgets the ghost's presence. Noticing his pleasure, the ghost cleverly dismisses the moment as frivolity and unimportant because, "He has spent but a few pounds of your mortal money: three or four perhaps. Is that so much that he deserves this praise?" (Stave Two), implying that Scrooge today, in his current state, would scoff at such a scene that couldn't be measured monetarily. Scrooge replies, "It isn't that, Spirit. He has the power to render us happy or unhappy; to make our service light or burdensome; a pleasure or a toil. Say that his power lies in words and looks; in things so slight and insignificant that it is impossible to add and count 'em up: what then? The happiness he gives, is quite as great as if it cost a fortune" (Stave Two). This moment is a foreshadowing of Scrooge's redemption because it is rather shocking to hear him admit that money is not the source of happiness. In the same way that Scrooge laments missing an opportunity to speak with the young caroler at his door earlier in his story, he now desires to speak with his lowly clerk, Bob Cratchit, realizing that he has placed money above Bob as a person and friend.

Christmas is indeed a season of senses. Our eyes search for light in the midst of darkness, our ears are tuned to sleigh bells and choirs, we taste and smell the "for a limited time only" gingerbreads and evergreen-scented candles. Probably the most underrated sense during Christmas season is the sense of touch. Have you ever done a "touch inventory"? Sometimes I do. I sit and think about what my hands have been doing all week. What is the thing I have most often touched? Usually the answer is plastic—my debit card, steering wheel, sippy cups, laptop, keys, and cell phone screen. The Christmas season has its own sense of touch, full of wrapping paper, tangled lights, waxy candles, and fir tree sap. What do your hands touch most often in December? I have to wonder, what does it say about our faith if we celebrate Christ's birth with plastic most often occupying our hands? How might our understanding of "God in the flesh" change if our hands were diligent in holding the hands of someone in need? What if our hands were busy preparing food with those for whom nutritious food is a luxury?

The real Christmas miracle comes not from what we are doing with our hands, but the fact that God himself was present in human form on earth. The miracle is that Jesus came to earth as fully God and fully man. He experienced life through all of the same five senses like we do. And what's maybe more mind-blowing is that our Savior had parents! Stanley Hauerwas writes:

> To be human is to be vulnerable, but to be a baby is to be vulnerable in a manner we spend a lifetime denying. Indeed Jesus was a baby refusing to forego the vulnerability that would climax in his crucifixion. And as such, Jesus was entrusted to the care of Mary and Joseph. They could not save him from the crucifixion, but they were indispensable agents to making his life possible.[2]

The Savior had parents. I've known this fact for quite a while, but it took on new meaning when I became a parent myself. God really surprises me sometimes, because when I think about the Savior having actual fallible, human parents, it sounds like a terrible plan. Because parents don't always get it right. Parents don't always keep their composure. Parents forget things—one day when Jesus was twelve years old, Mary and Joseph were traveling from Jerusalem, and it took them a full day to realize that Jesus wasn't with them. Some days I do all right in parenting, and other days I look up at the ceiling and say, "God, why can't I be better at this?" What was God thinking?

Faith is not a protective bubble against the dark places of the world. If it were, God would have never allowed himself to be raised by a pair of human, fallible, everyday, albeit blessed, parents.

The Incarnation—Christ becoming human—reveals the essence of faith, and that essence is the vulnerability of trust. Faith is not a protective bubble against the dark places of the world. If it were, God would have never allowed himself to be raised by a pair of human, fallible, everyday, albeit blessed, parents. In other words, Christmas reveals that God trusted humanity more than humanity has ever trusted itself.

Christmas is so mind-numbingly profound because God trusted humanity in order to save humanity. This thought causes me to read Romans 1:17 a bit differently. It says, "God's righteousness is being revealed in the gospel, from faithfulness for faith, as it is written, *The righteous person will live by faith.*" In other words, God had to trust in humanity in order to save humanity. What does it mean for God to trust in the broken, imperfect, screwed-up people of the world?

If God can trust in his creation in the midst of its imperfection, I guess I can, too. St. Gregory of Nazianzus once said, "What has not been assumed has not been healed; it is what is united to his divinity that is saved."[3] God entered into brokenness, God entered into an imperfect household, and God had eyes to cry and ears to hear the question, "Why Lord?" He had a mouth to taste the bitter herbs of poverty and oppression, and scarred hands offered to Thomas because that's what Thomas needed. And he had lips to challenge us and offer perpetual blessing—"Therefore, go and make disciples of all nations, baptizing them in the name of the Father and of the Son and of the Holy Spirit, teaching them to obey everything that I've commanded you. Look, I myself will be with you every day until the end of this present age" (Matthew 28:19-20).

What kind of music "moves" you during Christmas? What about those songs moves you or brings you closer to Jesus?

When you think about Jesus being fully human and fully man, what questions does that raise for you?

How might God be calling you to use your hands in a different way this Christmas?

THE ORDER OF CANDLES

"You fear the world too much," she answered, gently.
"All your other hopes have merged into the hope of being beyond the chance of its sordid reproach." (Stave Two)

In *Disney's A Christmas Carol*, starring Jim Carrey, the Ghost of Christmas Past appears as a candle. The apparition glows and floats about as a candle flickering in a gentle wind, guiding Scrooge along his journey. Candles and Christmastime seem to be an ordained pair. It's almost blasphemy to sing "Silent Night, Holy Night" without being burned from the wax of a small, white, reused candle. During the Advent season, each week many congregations light candles to represent Christ as God's light coming into the world, fulfilling our hope and expectation. Although the order in which the candles are lit can be different for different faith communities, I like to think of the candles as telling a story through peace, hope, love, and finally, joy. Just as the candle-like Ghost of Christmas Past takes Scrooge on a journey, these candles bring us on a journey unveiling the true meaning of Christ on earth—joy.

In many traditions, the first two candles we light represent *peace* and *hope*. These two words represent aspects of our faith that in some ways are complementary.

Christianity is filled with a holy tension—we live in a time between Christ's resurrection and the end, when heaven and earth will become one, and so we have to live in the middle. Ephesians 2:1-10, a letter traditionally attributed to the Apostle Paul, announced God's power over sin and death through our connection to Christ, yet amazingly, Paul wrote this letter from jail. It's safe to say that, from the outside looking in, things didn't look too good for Paul at that moment. Talking about how powerful God is while at the same time being held captive is not a great marketing strategy. Paul said, in essence, "I know how this looks, but have hope that God is continuing to reveal a mystery."

But if hope is an exercise in mystery, then peace is a challenge for proof. When we live in a godly hope for the future, it brings us together in peace. We can hope for lots of things for ourselves. But if I hope to win all the lottery prize money, it means I hope someone else won't. If I lust after absolute power, it means that I'm also hoping for someone else to be powerless. Peace, a complement of hope, is the sign that our hope is rooted in Christ and his kingdom.

There's more to the story, which is why we light a third candle for *love*. Peace means more than just no longer being at war. The Roman Empire established one of the most "peaceful" eras in human history, but that lack of conflict was earned through fear, power, and intimidation. Much like hope is connected with peace, peace must be rooted in love. Peace is the proof of Christian hope, and love is the sign that the peace is founded upon the gospel.

The last Advent candle we light is for *joy*. Advent, the waiting for Christ's birth, ends with joy because joy is something that only God can provide. Joy is a gift. It is not something you can do. It is not something you can earn. It can only be received from a loving and merciful God. "Joy to the world, the Lord is come," not "Joy to the world, because you have earned it." In order to understand joy, we must look prior to Jesus' birth. The Gospels first mention *joy* when Mary and Elizabeth meet in Luke 1. Mary comes from the hill country—in the north, the former kingdom of Israel—to visit Elizabeth in the south, the former kingdom of Judea. Now this may not seem like a significant detail, but when reading the Gospel of Luke, you must always pay attention to the setting. The important detail is this: Mary from the north meets Elizabeth from the south, and the child in Elizabeth's womb leaps. In this description, Luke is showing how God, through the birth of Christ, is uniting the old kingdom that was once divided over power struggles and foreign conquest. A child from the north and a child from the south indelibly linked by the good news of God. Through the birth of these two children, the kingdom is once again united under God, and the child leaps. Now, the text doesn't explicitly say that the child leapt *for joy*, but hold that thought.

If we fast-forward to Luke 6, we see Jesus preaching to the people, and he tells them, "Happy are you when people hate you, reject you, insult you, and condemn your name as evil because of the Human One. Rejoice when that happens! Leap for joy because you have a great reward in heaven" (vv. 22–23). Do you remember Luke 1:41 when John leapt in Elizabeth's womb when Mary arrived carrying Jesus in hers? This kind of leaping is only recorded twice in the entire New Testament. Once when the child leapt in the womb and the second when Jesus tells the crowd that they should leap for joy in the face of persecution because great is their reward in heaven. The child leaps in the womb not only because it foreshadows John's own persecution at the hands of Herod, but leaping for joy is a prophetic act symbolizing a gift from God that words just cannot describe. *Wait a second*, you might say, *do you mean that when we are hated and reviled, we should leap for joy?* Yes, because death is no longer the end of the story!

Back in Luke 2 we read: "Nearby shepherds were living in the fields, guarding their sheep at night. The Lord's angel stood before them, the Lord's glory shone around them, and they were terrified" (Luke 2:8-9). The line between fear and joy is as thin as a moment is short. Consider the wealthy man who came to Jesus in Luke 18, asking what he needed to do to inherit the kingdom of God. The man said that he had followed the law and he had done no wrong, so what was left for him to do? Jesus said, "Go, sell what you have, give

73

to the poor, and follow me." The man walked away in sorrow, for he loved his money more than his life. He was on the doorstep of great joy, he was looking into the very face of Christ, but he walked away afraid. The shepherds who saw the angel were also filled with fear, but the angel transformed their fear into joy because, unlike the man who walked away in sorrow, they remained to hear the good news. "The angel said, 'Don't be afraid! Look! I bring good news to you—wonderful, joyous news for all people. Your savior is born today in David's city. He is Christ the Lord' " (Luke 2:10-11).

But there is even more that the Gospel of Luke has to tell us about joy. Fast-forward to Luke 24. After Jesus' death, the women came to the tomb to anoint his body, and they were met by two men in dazzling clothes. The women came with sorrow, which quickly turned to fear, just like the shepherds. The men announced that Christ was risen and the women quickly turned to go back to the apostles. Jesus appeared to the apostles and those who were walking to Emmaus, and then we get the point: "[Jesus] led them out as far as Bethany, where he lifted his hands and blessed them. As he blessed them, he left them and was taken up to heaven. They worshipped him and returned to Jerusalem overwhelmed with joy. And they were continuously in the temple praising God" (vv. 50–53).

Joy is the steadfast assurance that God is with us.

Joy is the steadfast assurance that God is with us. You can't do anything to earn this great gift, but like the story of the rich young ruler, we can, by holding on to our wealth, forget that the gifts we receive are from God. So, open your hands and your heart to an experience of the divine that words fall short to describe. The best word we have for this experience is not *peace*, even though being at peace with each other creates the setting and atmosphere for God. The best word we have for this experience is not *hope*, though hope points us in the right direction. The best word we have for this experience is not even *love*, though love is the fundamental nature of God who raised Christ from the dead. The best word we have for this experience is *joy* because it is a gift from God that makes you leap. It is a gift from God that allows you to rise above persecution. It is a gift from God experienced when you come face to face with the risen Lord. It is the steadfast assurance that God is with us!

What holds you back from accepting God's gift of joy?

How have you experienced joy this Advent season? How would you describe God's presence in your life?

Based on your walk with Christ, in what order would you prefer to light the Advent candles?

REFLECTION:
PICTURES OF THE PAST

"Why, it's old Fezziwig! Bless his heart; it's
Fezziwig alive again!... [Mr. Fezziwig] has the
power to render us happy or unhappy; to make our
service light or burdensome; a pleasure or a toil."
(Stave Two)

Return the joy of your salvation to me
and sustain me with a willing spirit.
(Psalm 51:12)

The Ghost of Christmas Past took Scrooge on a journey through his memories, the way you or I might flip through a photo album or Facebook news feed. Some snapshots of Scrooge's past were joyful, such as the memories of his old boss, Mr. Fezziwig; while other photos reminded him of things he would rather forget.

To say that my wife, Christie, enjoys taking pictures would be a gross understatement. We have an entire room in our home devoted to scrapbooking. (At least, we used to until baby number four came along.) The room had two external hard drives filled with original and edited photos, multiple camera lenses for multiple occasions, four albums set aside exclusively for our family's Walt Disney World vacations, and picture frames everywhere. Christie's obsession with photography is matched only by my penchant for anything Disney. It was a joyous day when we discovered that our personal eccentricities overlapped.

Some of our favorite photos were taken at Christmas. However, as Scrooge learned, not all Christmas memories are happy. One year, our Christmas tree toppled over when we weren't at home, smashing nearly all our glass ornaments, many of which were reminders of family and friends. It was a difficult day. So we did what we often do when we experience sadness—we opened the photo albums and remembered the happy times.

While we flipped through the memories, we came across a picture of our first real Christmas tree. I lovingly call it the "Bethlehem Supernova" because of all the lights strung around the tree's small frame. We had a great laugh, which helped us realize that even though the tree and ornaments are special to us, they pale in comparison to our relationships with God and each other, which after all are what the tree and ornaments represent.

Scrooge's unhappy memories were not so easily set aside. Near the end of his journey with the Ghost of Christmas Past, he relived a time when he and his sweetheart, Belle, discovered there was no longer any overlap in their divergent lives. Before leaving him, she said of their failed relationship, "A very, very brief time, and you will dismiss the recollection of it, gladly, as an unprofitable dream, from which it happened well that you awoke. May you be happy in the life you have chosen!" (Stave Two). Scrooge was filled with pain at the recollection of that last meeting with Belle.

Scrooge never regained Belle's love, but reliving the memory eventually moved him to compassion toward those who know the pain of brokenness. Do you know heartache? Do you have painful memories? How might God be calling you to use those past snapshots in the future? How can God transform those memories into future blessings for you and for others?

Gracious God, you know our past faults and failures because you are always with us. By the power of your Spirit, transform our heartache into acts of mercy and justice for your children today and every tomorrow. Sustain us with your presence, and remind us of your salvation offered through Christ. Amen.

CHAPTER THREE

THE LIFE OF CHRISTMAS PRESENT

"Come in!" exclaimed the Ghost. "Come in! and know me better, man!" (Stave Three)

Maybe you've heard the idiom, "There's no time like the present." I find thinking about time fascinating because "the present"—this moment, right now—is so fleeting. There is, in fact, no time *in* the present because the moment I start thinking about the present, it's already in the past. Indeed, "there's no time like the present," because it can't be measured or quantified. It's over before it's begun. I've also heard that the present is called *the present* because it is a gift. This is true in the sense that present is where all of the action is!

ADVENT WEEK 3: LOVE

This week we light the candle of Love. Christina Rossetti, a late-nineteenth-century poet, wrote, "Love came down at Christmas, love all lovely, Love Divine; Love was born at Christmas, star and angels gave the sign."[1] Jesus was the fully divine (love came down) and fully human (love was born) Son of God. Making sense of Jesus' full divinity and full humanity existing in the same place and same time is confusing. The Nicene Creed attempts to spell it out saying: "We believe in one Lord, Jesus Christ, the only Son of God, eternally begotten of the Father, God from God, Light from Light, true God from true God, begotten, not made, of one being with the Father."[2] It's almost funny that the best way we can describe this cornerstone of our faith is to say that Christ is of the same substance as God, or in other words, whatever God is, Christ is, too.

The point is that love both "came down," and "was born," because love is who God is. God is the creator of all things seen and unseen. God is full of majesty and glory. God's presence also lives intimately within us, closer to us than the air we breathe. When we learn to love God and love one another, I am convinced that what we share is the very presence of the divine. Yes, it can be confusing, and there is a tension when trying to explain it, but love lies at the center of it all. We light the candle of Love as a sign of the beautiful mystery of God's love.

Gracious God, whose love came down and put on flesh to walk among us, help us to accept and share your presence, so that the world might know your love. In the name of the Father and of the Son and of the Holy Spirit. Amen.

Another popular idiom is to say that someone "tells it like it is." When people say this, what they usually mean is they agree with what has been said. At least, I've rarely heard someone say, "He tells it like it is, and he is totally wrong." The interesting thing about telling it like it is, so to speak, is that we can never be completely objective when observing *it,* whatever *it* happens to be. We will always, however small, only be able to tell it like we see it.

The Ghost of Christmas Present is about to take Scrooge on a journey, offering Scrooge a window into the way things are that he could not experience by himself. If anyone can tell it like it is, the Ghost of Christmas Present certainly can.

Want, Need, Wear, Read

It was his own room. There was no doubt about that. But it had undergone a surprising transformation.

(Stave Three)

The Ghost of Christmas Past's presence seemed to Scrooge like a dream. It hovered near his bed, ethereal and confusing, like hearing a strange sound in the middle of the night and then realizing you left the television on. In contrast, the Ghost of Christmas Present is appropriately named, as his interaction feels real, present, and tangible.

As Scrooge awakens from sleep and realizes it's time for the next ghost to appear, the clock strikes one but no spirit appears. It is several minutes before Scrooge sees light shining under the door and is wooed by the Ghost of Christmas Present into another room, a room transformed with signs of life. Holly and berries adorn the walls, the fireplace roars with heat, and a bounty of food covers every surface. The Ghost towers above him with a booming and joyful voice. The Ghost of Christmas Past had felt intimate yet distant, and the visions he had shown were fleeting and separated from Scrooge himself. Scrooge had tried to interact with the people from his memory, but he could not, leaving him with a detached experience (not unlike spending time with a friend who will never put his phone down). But now, with the Ghost of Christmas Present, Scrooge can feel the warmth of the fire and smell the turkey on the table. Scrooge may have questioned whether his experience with the first spirit was real, but now there is little question.

The laughter, warmth, food, and decorations of Christmas remind us of God's ever-present abundance. God is always present and always offers us what we need. Scrooge's senses come alive in the "realness" of this vision. Why? Because the present is the only part of time that feels real. The past is a memory, and the future is a dream, but the present is *now*, and *now* is when everything happens. Every word of love we share, every meal we enjoy, every song we've heard were all experienced in the now. The past and future are simply *nows* that you have either experienced or will experience. That's why I like to say that God lives in an eternal now. It's all now to God because God is independent of time as we know it. He is eternal and omnipotent, which is a concept that's hard for us to understand. But think about it like taking a long road trip—you travel from one point to the next, from mountains to valleys, but the earth is always under your feet.

Not only is God always with us, but God always offers us what we need. Unfortunately we often confuse our needs with wants. Sin causes us to be afraid we won't have enough, so we buy more food than we need, more clothing than we can wear, and more shelter than we can keep clean. A fourth-century monk, Basil of Caesarea, once said, "This bread which you have set aside is the bread of the hungry; this garment you have locked away is the clothing of the naked; those shoes which you let rot are the shoes of him who is barefoot; those riches you have hoarded are the riches of the poor."[3] God always provides enough. The problem is we are afraid it isn't enough. This story is as old as the birth of humanity. God offered the man and the woman every tree in the garden except one, but their fear of not having enough transformed desire for the Creator of the fruit to the fruit itself, and Jesus came to unwind that misguided desire that we still struggle with today.

God's gifts are truly abundant, but sometimes we share this abundance in unhelpful ways. We are a "too much" people, like some of the ancient Israelites who were in the wilderness with Moses. The Lord told Moses to announce to the people that God would cause manna to rain down from heaven to provide for their need. He told them to take only enough, but some of the people collected more than they needed. The abundance spoiled and rotted (Exodus 16:19-20). It's a tired sermon to hear that we spend too much and eat too much and spend too much, especially during the holiday season. As Pastor Mike Slaughter writes, "Christmas is not *your* birthday!"[4] But what we are supposed to do about it? Should we skip the stores altogether during Christmas? Should we just buy less?

I will say that, as a parent, it is certainly tough to see Christmas list items, knowing that they won't be showing up under the tree on Christmas morning. So we started a new tradition in our family— when our kids put together their Christmas lists, we ask them to write down four things: something they want, something they need, something to wear, and something to read. The kids can write down whatever they like. Of course their "somethings they want" list is quite long, but they know that after Santa's reindeer leave, there will be four things (plus one—Santa often leaves something for them to share) under the tree. Now, this plan isn't perfect, and it doesn't work for everyone.

Here's our thinking: we get them something they want because, as Christians, we should want to be near God, to have a desire to be with God. Desire is not a bad thing. We should long for God as the deer longs for streams of water (Psalm 42:1). Too often this desire manifests itself during the holiday season as coveting, which is rooted in desire, but it is a desire for what your neighbor has. We also get our children something they need to remind them that we are always in need of God's grace and forgiveness. Want coupled with desire reflects Philippians 4:19—"And my God will fully satisfy every need of yours according to his riches in glory in Christ Jesus" (NRSV). God satisfies our needs, but also leaves us wanting more. This is why when the author of Psalm 23 trusted that God was with him, his cup overflowed (Psalm 23:5). Our children also receive something to wear. Clothing, for good or ill, says something about us. It is a way to tell every passerby a little bit of who we consider ourselves to be. As Christians we should wear the humility, kindness, and generosity of Christ (Romans 13:14).

Thankfully, our children are still excited when they get something to read on Christmas morning. Education is important for the "renewing of your mind" (Romans 12:2), and reading Scripture daily is a practice I hope my children never grow out of. I have been astounded at the transformation I have seen from friends who begin to read Scripture daily. Almost always our conversations begin with, "I never knew that..." or "It's so interesting that..." or "This really helped me understand..."

Finally, the kids receive one gift to share to remind us that church is where we learn to share our prayers, presence, gifts, service, and witness. Early in the church's history, the Book of Acts tells us that those first believers shared all of their material goods, so that everyone's needs were met (Acts 2:44). As our children grow older, I pray they will come to realize the significance of the gifts they receive, and that ultimately it's not about the presents under the tree, but the presence of each other. As parents, we are learning as we go. It's not perfect, but we have found that is has been a great way, in the midst of the chaos of Christmas morning, to remember God's gift of Jesus.

Abundance can certainly get out of hand during the holiday season. When we surround ourselves with stuff rather than Spirit, we find ourselves getting angry that Starbucks's cups aren't Christian enough, or we become defensive when someone at the grocery store wishes us "Happy Holidays" instead of "Merry Christmas." We begin to think that there is a war on Christmas while forgetting that there are actual wars happening across the world.

Jesus' birth is the eye of a storm that continues to turn the world upside down. He came so that we might discover and share abundant and everlasting life.

Jesus' birth is the eye of a storm that continues to turn the world upside down. He came so that we might discover and share abundant and everlasting life. Jesus was born in the lowest place on earth, and the angels worshiped God, saying, "Glory to God in the highest heaven" (Luke 2:14 NRSV). Through Jesus, God has reconciled everything, from the depths of the earth to the farthest star in the sky. So fill your cup with good things this season and share God's goodness with the world!

What are some ways you continue the Christmas spirit all year long?

How do you share the Christmas story with your family through the gifts you offer?

GOOD NEWS, FOR SOME

"There was nothing very cheerful in the climate or the town, and yet was there an air of cheerfulness abroad that the clearest summer air and brightest summer sun might have endeavoured to diffuse in vain." (Stave Three)

As soon as Scrooge begins to travel with the Ghost of Christmas Present, he notices how dreadful the town is. The houses look bleak, as the wintry weather seems to emphasize the chilly disposition of everything he sees. It is not that the streets were full of squalor; rather the grayness of it all left little room for good tidings and the usual cheerfulness we have come to know during the holiday season. Surprisingly, however, there is a glimmer of an unexpected happiness. Dickens writes, "There was nothing very cheerful in the climate or the town, and yet was there an air of cheerfulness abroad that the clearest summer air and brightest summer sun might have endeavoured to diffuse in vain" (Stave Three). He notices that the people shoveling the snow are gleeful, the produce in the shops is radiant, and the shopkeepers joyful. It's almost as if there are two stories happening at the same time—joy and pain, frivolity and hardship, abundance and scarcity.

This must have been what Jesus' first night on earth was like. "Silent Night, Holy Night" invites us to sing, "Radiant beams from thy holy face with the dawn of redeeming grace,"[5] but too often we forget that Christ's light was shining upon the poverty of a family who could find no room in the inn. Scrooge was, maybe for the first time, beginning to see the spirit of Christmas for what it is—a glimmer of hope in a hurting world.

The Christmas celebration seems all to short, doesn't it? For months we gather lists and coupons and decorations and reservations, and in the blink of an eye, the twenty-sixth arrives. "Merry Christmas" is exchanged for "Happy New Year," and the Christmas cheer of figgy pudding gives way for the luck and prosperity of steamed cabbage and black-eyed peas. The Christmas spirit seems short-lived, especially if we are brave enough to worship on the Sunday after Christmas. My second sermon ever as a pastor in a local church was on the Sunday after Christmas on what I call "National Associate Pastor Sunday," or NAPS for short (because that's usually what the rest of the congregation is doing that particular Sunday). It's hard enough to preach your sophomore sermon, but to make matters worse, the text made me sick even to read. In the Revised Common Lectionary, the Gospel reading the Sunday after Christmas is often Matthew 2:16-18, or what is commonly known as "The Slaughter of the Innocents."

When Herod knew the magi had fooled him, he grew very angry. He sent soldiers to kill all the children in Bethlehem and in all the surrounding territory who were two years old and younger, according to the time that he had learned from the magi. This fulfilled the word spoken through Jeremiah the prophet:

> *A voice was heard in Ramah,*
> *weeping and much grieving.*
> *Rachel weeping for her children,*
> *and she did not want to be comforted,*
> *because they were no more.*

The organ pipes are still warm from our heralded "Hark! the Herald Angels Sing," and next comes a terrible story of innocent children being slaughtered out of fear from what this Christ Child is bringing into the world. The Christmas celebration is over.

Do we have the audacity to sing about joy in the midst of unspeakable atrocities? What child is this that we would sing, "Glory to God in the highest"? Then before our next breath, our lips prepare to remember Jeremiah, saying, "Rachel is weeping for her children, she will not be comforted." Jesus is still very small when Joseph is warned in a dream to take the child and his mother to Egypt in order to escape certain death. That evening, in the midst of nightfall, the Holy Family left for the land of Egypt. This image of Egypt is one of the most powerful in all of Scripture. Egypt is the land of plenty. The Nile Delta is some of the most fertile land in the Middle East, allowing Egypt to have plentiful harvests, booming economy, a powerful army, and enough leisure to construct the pyramids—the only wonder of the ancient world still in existence. It is the land where Abram ventured to escape famine. It is the land where Joseph, Jacob's son, saved his brothers from famine. It is the land where the ancient Israelites flourished and became plentiful according to God's commandment, "be fruitful and multiply." Yet Egypt is also the land in which the ancient Israelites were enslaved because they had become so numerous. Pharaoh's fear of losing power transformed Egypt from a land of prosperity for the Israelites into a land of oppression, a land of bondage, a land of slavery, a land of darkness.

Now, with the birth of the Christ Child, Israel is experiencing barbarity at the hands of Herod. Herod, like Pharaoh, is afraid of this child, or more specifically, he is afraid of losing power. The second chapter of Matthew begins with wise men from the east who asked, "Where is this child who is to become King of the Jews?" When King Herod heard this, he became frightened, but what is even more provocative than Herod's fear is that Scripture said all Jerusalem shared in the king's fear. All of Jerusalem was afraid. I don't know exactly what Jerusalem feared, but I am certain that fear is infectious. It spreads more quickly and is more dangerous than any disease.

In Scott Bader-Saye's, *Following Jesus in a Culture of Fear*, he writes about a 2004 *USA Today* editorial, which depicted a life tragically overwhelmed by fear. The author described herself as a "security mom," representing the newest fashionable mom-bloc of voters. She writes:

> I am what this year's election pollsters call a "security mom." I'm married with two young children. I own a gun, and I vote....The Sept. 11th 2001 terrorist attacks shook me out of my Generation X stupor. Unlike Hollywood and *The New York Times* and the ivory tower, I have not settled back casually into a Sept. 10th way of life. I have studied the faces on the FBI's most-wanted-terrorists list. When I ride the train, I watch for suspicious packages in empty seats. When I am on the highways, I pay attention to large trucks and tankers. I make my husband take his cellphone with him everywhere—even on a quick milk run or on a walk to the community pool. We have educated our 4-year-old daughter about Osama bin Laden and Saddam Hussein. She knows that there are bad men in the world trying to kill Americans everywhere.... [A]t night, we ask God to bless our troops as they risk their lives trying to kill the bad men before they kill us.[6]

Now I know that Christianity struggles with pacifism and war and the debate over what a just war looks like. When our daily prayer becomes, "kill them before they kills us," it is a moment when fear has won. It is the moment when fear has invaded our hearts, our souls, our minds to the point of paralysis, when we can do nothing but fear. I can't help but think that "kill them before they kill us," was precisely Herod's prayer when he heard the news that a new king had been born. Herod's fear plunged himself and all of Jerusalem into a frenzy so chaotic that an angel of the Lord came to Joseph in a dream and said "get out."

I don't feel that the Holy Family fled Bethlehem in order to avoid danger. If this is so, we are left with difficult, maybe unanswerable, questions about who God is. There seems to be more to the story than God wanting to protect Jesus and not the other children in Bethlehem. The Holy Family journeys into Egypt—the Christ Child travels to the land where his ancestors were enslaved, the land of bondage and oppression, the land that throughout the Old Testament represented everything that God was not. Egypt was more than a powerful image to the Jewish people—to them it represented the opposite of God. Time and time again we see phrases such as, "I am the LORD your God who brought you out of Egypt" (Exodus 20:2), and "out of Egypt I called my son" (Hosea 11:1). Here the Christ Child enters this land of oppression, not for protection, but because Egypt itself needs to be redeemed. See, in this story, Egypt is transformed from a land of oppression to a land of refuge, from a land of bondage, to a land which cradled the Child who would deliver God's children from slavery to sin and death. The God of Abraham, Isaac, and Jacob redeemed Egypt so that it could once again be a blessing as it had been for Abraham, Isaac, and Jacob. In other words, Christ, in his infancy transforms Egypt, this ancient symbol of hate and fear, into a symbol of hope and resurrection.

This is what happens when you let Christ in. Christ transforms fear itself into an embodiment of hope.

This is what happens when you let Christ in. Christ transforms fear itself into an embodiment of hope. If Christ can redeem Egypt, then what are the possibilities? On Tuesday, August 16, 2005, Brother Roger, the founder of a religious community in Taizé, France, was stabbed to death during a prayer service. While the brothers were praying, a Romanian woman emerged from the congregation and murdered the ninety-year-old man in his wheelchair. Surely this would be grounds for metal detectors and bag searchers and plastic bags for all of your lotions and liquids, right? But Otto Selles, a professor at Calvin College, visited the Taizé community shortly after Brother Roger's murder, and wrote,

> "Nothing at Taizé has changed. There is no security..." [Brother Jean-Marie told Selles], "the community is very, very united." After the visit I realized why the Brothers would probably never put metal detectors in the Church of Reconciliation—their sense of spiritual security and calm goes miles deeper than most of us would like to admit. At the funeral service for Brother Roger [they] didn't shy from mentioning [the name of his murderer] and committing her to God's forgiveness.... Set on such a path of both reconciliation and truth, Taize continues to offer a "parable of community" to France and the rest of the world.[7]

When fear grabs hold of our souls, as it did King Herod's, our prayer can quickly become "kill them before they kill us," but when Christ enters into our soul, our prayer is transformed into a prayer calling for God's forgiveness of our enemies. How do we react when we are faced with Bethlehem—those places of suffering? Some say Bethlehem is an ancient place where countless children were slaughtered at the hands of a fearful king. Some say *Bethlehem* is on the eastern coast of Africa, in Sudan, where the vulnerable often do not survive. Some say *Bethlehem* is outside the Green Zone in Baghdad, where suicide bombers are a daily reminder of evil. Some say *Bethlehem* is a shopping mall where a young man ended innocent lives before taking his own. Scripture says Bethlehem was the place in which God came to earth, veiled in flesh, in order to save God's people. This place of torment and suffering is precisely where God chose to be born so that God, through Christ, could transform tears of sadness into tears of joy.

Just as Christ went down into Egypt to transform Egypt from oppressor to cradle of redemption, God came down to Bethlehem in the form of a child in order to transform the world from a kingdom of fear into the kingdom of heaven. How do we react when we are faced with the *Bethlehems* of our lives? The hymn "O Little Town of Bethlehem" becomes rather haunting when you pause to ponder the words. The city is still. There is a dreamless sleep. The stars are silent, yet moving as if apathetic toward Herod's violence. Is it possible for culture to mimic Scripture? For it was in Bethlehem that the hopes and fears of all the years were met. It was the place where hope won!

> O little town of Bethlehem, how still we see thee lie;
> above thy deep and dreamless sleep the silent stars go by.
> Yet in thy dark streets shineth the everlasting light;
> the hopes and fears of all the years are met in thee tonight.[8]

What are some areas where God wants to transform your fear into redemption?

How do you define "Bethlehem"? Where do you see suffering happening?

What makes you fearful during this time of year?

CRATCHITS AND CRUTCHES

> *He told me, coming home, that he hoped the people saw*
> *him in the church, because he was a cripple, and it might*
> *be pleasant to them to remember upon Christmas Day,*
> *who made lame beggars walk, and blind men see.*
>
> (Stave Three)

Scrooge is traveling with the Ghost of Christmas Present when the church bells ring out. As townsfolk leave their homes to gather in the sanctuary, the spirit begins to sprinkle incense upon the families' meals as a means of blessing their food. As Scrooge is perplexed why the spirit is offering more incense to some and less to others, the spirit replies without reservation that the poor need it the most. The spirit's simple gesture offers us a moment to pause and consider how God works within the world.

Sometimes we think justice means that everyone should receive the same, but this doesn't seem to be the gospel that Jesus proclaimed. I've seen a cartoon that explains this well: imagine a six-foot-tall fence, and three people of varying heights trying to see what is on the other side. One person is six-foot-three, the other five-foot-seven, and the other four-foot even. Let's say that each person receives a one-foot crate to use in order to see over the fence. The tallest person is well over the fence, but he can no longer hold on to the fence to keep his balance. The shortest person still cannot see over the fence. The person in the middle is holding steady, enjoying the view. This may represent equality in the sense that they all received the same crate, but this is hardly justice.

Throughout Scripture, God's justice involves a lifting up of the lowly.

Throughout Scripture, God's justice involves a lifting up of the lowly, not a divine mandate that all receive the same. In Matthew 20:1-16, Jesus offered a parable about what God's kingdom looks like on earth. Early in the morning, a landowner hired laborers to work in his field for a day's wage. The workers agreed and got to work. Later in the day, the same landowner hired additional staff. Just before the whistle blew at the end of the day, the landowner still hired more workers. At the end of the day, the landowner paid alll of the workers the same daily wage. On the one hand this looks like equality because everyone is receiving the same salary, but what happens at the end of the parable reveals that this parable is about an extravagant God who favors the lowly. At the end of the day, the landowner paid those who worked the least first. When they received a full day's wage, the workers who had been in the field all day become angry.

> Now when the first came, they thought they would receive more; but each of them also received the usual daily wage. And when they received it, they grumbled against the landowner, saying, "These last worked only one hour, and you have made them *equal* to us who have borne the burden of the day and the scorching heat." But he replied to one of them, "Friend, I am doing you no wrong; did you not agree with me for the usual daily wage? Take what belongs to you and go; I choose to give to this last the same as I give to you. Am I not allowed to do what I choose with what belongs to me? Or are you envious because I am generous?" So the last will be first, and the first will be last.
>
> (Matthew 20:10-16, NRSV, *emphasis mine*)

One could argue that the landowner was completely unfair. The workers who invested more time in the field should have been offered more compensation, but this parable is not about economy or fair labor practices or our GDP. In other words, it's not that all of the laborers received the same crate; rather all of them were offered an opportunity to see over the fence. The parable is about God searching all day to invite people into the vineyard, into the church, and into communion with each other.

Luke 15 offers three other parables about God's justice toward the lost and the lowly. In the first parable a shepherd left ninety-nine sheep alone to search for the one that was lost. Jesus asked a rhetorical question to the grumbling Pharisees saying, "Suppose someone among you had one hundred sheep and lost one of them. Wouldn't he leave the other ninety-nine in the pasture and search for the lost one until he finds it?" (Luke 15:4). The question was rhetorical because none of them would risk so much for such a minimal return. Jesus continued saying, "Or what woman, if she owns ten silver coins and loses one of them, won't light a lamp and sweep the house, searching her home carefully until she finds it?" (Luke 15:8). We have an easier time accepting this parable because looking for lost money seems a worthy venture, until one realizes that spending all day looking for the coin meant none of the other household labor gets done. Wouldn't you just cut your losses and move on? The third parable in Luke 15 was about a man who had two sons. When the younger son, who squandered his inheritance on "loose living," was welcomed home with a party, the older brother (or dare I say, the laborer who had been in the field all day) became angry at such a weak and foolish gesture.

A rejoicing justice is at the heart of this kingdom.

It might seem wasteful to our contemporary ears, but these parables are not about making a profit other than profiting the celebration of what was lost is found. A rejoicing justice is at the heart of this kingdom. In each parable, all we are asked to do is rejoice with the shepherd, the woman, and the father when the lost had been found, which is why Jesus told this parable in front of the Pharisees who were grumbling because of the many sinners in his presence.

When Scrooge questions the spirit's motives, almost blaming the spirit for the cultural command to rest on the Sabbath (by closing the shops), the spirit offers a damning judgment, saying that humanity has performed terrible things in the name of "his kin." If Scrooge is looking to blame someone, he should blame humanity. When the poor are vilified or assumed to be lazy, when the only solution to systemic poverty is working harder in a system that favors the prosperous, when our mission and outreach only consist of a meal for the poor instead of a place at the table with the poor, we risk God's kingdom being foreign to us. We risk being angry with God's lavish grace. We risk cutting our losses with the ninety-nine sheep and missing God's kingdom that rests with the one. In other words, not everything done in God's name is something God would bless, or as Jesus said in Matthew 7:21—"Not everybody who says to me, 'Lord, Lord,' will get into the kingdom of heaven. Only those who do the will of my Father who is in heaven will enter."

Sometimes our Christmas missions miss the mark. We are so quick to offer the less fortunate gifts for stockings rather than a place at our table and room in our lives because gifts in a stocking are the extent of our limited vision of what Christ being born means. It's not that we never offer gifts during Christmas, but what do these gifts say about our understanding of God coming into the world? Maybe the gift we can offer this year is the gift of silence so that those without a voice in our community may speak? Maybe the gift we offer this year is asking difficult questions of why so many children are on the Salvation Army's stocking list? Maybe our gift is offering incense to others before we pour it upon our own tree? We often like to say that it's better to give than to receive, but do we follow through with that? What might we offer to the world to bring about real change?

Eventually the ghost takes Scrooge to the home of his counting clerk, Bob Cratchit. The Cratchits are a simple family who share great faith, which seems to go hand in hand more than some realize. Scrooge overhears Bob talking about taking his young son, Tiny Tim, to church that evening, saying, "He told me, coming home, that he hoped the people saw him in the church, because he was a cripple, and it might be pleasant to them to remember upon Christmas Day, who made lame beggars walk, and blind men see" (Stave Three). Amen!

What are some ways you might "share incense" with those in need?

I've heard it said that "Do not take the Lord's name in vain," from Exodus 20:7, means that we should not do in God's name the things that God would not bless. How have you seen God's name taken in vain?

Would Tiny Tim be seen in your congregation? If so, how would he be received?

EYES TO SEE

There never was such a goose. (Stave Three)

The Cratchits' Christmas dinner is an exercise in noticing blessings. "There never was such a goose," Bob says at his meager table (Stave Three). Some might overlook the beautiful bounty of their simple meal, but the paltry abundance is not lost on the Cratchits, who know the difficulty of poverty all too well.

It is easy to get distracted with the decorations, lights, and festive music of Christmas; but at its heart, the first Nativity is a story born out of poverty, where scarcity is transformed into abundance by a God who will stop at nothing to be with us. It's easy to get wrapped up in the magnificent "Gloria, Gloria in excelsis Deo," and forget that the angels are singing to shepherds. If we read Luke's Christmas story carefully, bringing out the fine china for a Christmas Eve meal might even leave us a bit uncomfortable. Of course the Christmas story is about a baby—two actually, according to Luke's Gospel— but the story begins before Jesus is born, and the setting in which Luke's Gospel takes places tells a story all its own.

When we were pregnant with our first child, my wife and I both read books about pregnancy. Her book was titled *What to Expect When You're Expecting,* which should be more accurately titled *Paranoia.* This book provides the worst-case scenarios for pregnancy, saying things like, "Eat a lot of fish, but don't eat too much because if you do..." then it goes on to list different birth defects. It says, "Be sure to exercise, but don't do too much, because if you do..." followed by another list. My book was very different. It said things like, "This week your baby is the size of a buffalo wing," and "This week the baby will react to light if you shine a flashlight at the baby's mother." So while my wife is calorie counting, I find myself staring lovingly at a buffalo wing in one hand with a flashlight in the other. Having a baby is a very strange experience. It is wonderful. It is miraculous. But it is strange. The baby in the womb actually reacts to the outside world. It can hear what we say. It reacts to light and different foods. It seems like the baby is already here, but not yet. The baby is here, alive, but not yet born.

At its heart, the first Nativity is a story born out of poverty, where scarcity is transformed into abundance by a God who will stop at nothing to be with us.

Luke begins his Nativity story with, "In those days Caesar Augustus declared that everyone throughout the empire should be enrolled in the tax lists. This first enrollment occurred when Quirinius governed Syria" (Luke 2:1-2). Luke wants to make sure that Jesus' birth narrative is situated in a specific time and place. This is the story of when God entered into human history, not with thunder and lightning, but with a chorus of angels and lowly shepherds and a wandering family placing their newborn child in a feeding trough. *In those days*... Luke wants us to know that this is God becoming incarnate, in a real time and a real place, with hands and eyes, and needing constant care, unthinkable humility for the Creator of all that is, seen and unseen.

There's a transformation happening. Jesus was born in Bethlehem, which means "house of bread."[9] Jesus is the Bread of Life, placed in a feeding trough because it is Christ upon which we feed to be filled with grace. Jesus grew up in Nazareth, which means "new shoot,"[10] because Jesus is the fulfillment of prophecy rooted in God's Word, but also the new way God is choosing to be with God's people. Jesus saw his final days in Jerusalem, the "city of peace,"[11] because it is through the cross that we find our peace with God and with each other. Jesus' birth means "those days" are passing away, and "this day" will be with us forever!

The angels appeared in the heavens, not saying, "In those days . . ."—rather they proclaimed, "To you *is* born *this* day in the city of David a Savior, who *is* the Messiah, the Lord" (Luke 2:11 NRSV, *emphasis mine*). *In those days* the palace ruled the world, but on *this day* the world is being turned upside down. *In those days* the shepherds were less than unimportant, but on *this day*, the shepherds received a gift of the kingdom of God! *In those days* we simply read about a miracle. On *this day* we expect one. *In those days* we tried to make our traditions and material gifts perfect. On *this day* we let go of the anxiety of making things perfect so that we can make room for a perfect God. *In those days* our Christmas list was full of material things for friends, family, coworkers. On *this day* our list contains what Jesus wants. It is his birthday, after all. Jesus wants the proclamation of good news, release, recovery, freedom, and favor. *In those days* we worried about what's under the tree instead of the tree itself. On *this day* we see clearly the Giver of Life.

The angels' proclamation is timeless. When we read the angels' words, "To you is born this day in the city of David a Savior, who is the Messiah, the Lord" (Luke 2:11 NRSV), we speak a timeless truth, making Christ's presence with us an ever-present reality. It's a word that becomes timeless because it is always in the present, which is the place God resides, the place where God lives. *In those days* Christmas was seen as our birthday. On *this day* may we remember that this is the night we celebrate Jesus' birth.

The announcement was made to shepherds, and maybe this is the key to understanding what God is doing—God is favoring the poor with this grand announcement, and this should give us pause in the way we often think about poverty. Sam Wells, in his book *A Nazareth Manifesto*, writes about how poverty is not a problem that needs to be fixed, where the "haves" offer the "have-nots" a solution to their trying predicament so they might "better themselves." He writes:

> We do not sit and have coffee with a homeless person because we are trying to solve their problem—we do so because we want to receive the wealth of wisdom, humanity, and grace that God has to give us through them. We are not the source of their salvation. . . . Our every effort is to enjoy their being, and share our own, rather than change their reality assuming a script we have imposed from elsewhere.[12]

Why did God send the angels to the shepherds? God delivers the good news to the shepherds, not because they were best equipped to spread the news, or that they were nearby and it was convenient; it is because God was already there, with the unlikely.

God delivers the good news to the shepherds, not because they were best equipped to spread the news, or that they were nearby and it was convenient; it is because God was already there, with the unlikely.

Near the end of Jesus' life, a woman anointed Jesus' feet with expensive perfume, which angered many of the disciples, who thought it was a waste. Jesus replied, "You always have the poor with you, but you won't always have me" (Matthew 26:11). This sounds almost like poverty should be ignored because it as certain as "death and taxes," but Jesus was quoting Deuteronomy 15:11— "Poor persons will never disappear from the earth. That's why I'm giving you this command: you must open your hand generously to your fellow Israelites, to the needy among you, and to the poor who live with you in your land." This is not quid pro quo, this is a call to action! God's announcement to the shepherds reveals there is even more to this command than meets the eye. God doesn't offer them good news as a means of opening a divine hand to their neediness; it is a revelation that Christ is with them, joining them in poverty, not because there was no means of affluence, but because poverty is near God's heart.

And so we pray that God would move our hearts forward from *those days*, when we thought this night was about us, to *this day* and we proclaim Jesus' wish list of good news, release, recovery, freedom, and favor. We do this because this is God's story, and through grace, it is our own.

How have you been living in those days?

How might God be calling you to live this day?

GOD BLESS US, EVERY ONE

[Grace] is free in all to whom it is given.[13]

Tiny Tim's "God bless Us, Every One" (Stave Five) is one of the most iconic phrases in pop literature. (You almost have to say it in a British accent to get the best effect.) What if we modeled our Advent and Christmas comings and goings as if we actually believe that God has already blessed everyone? Charles Wesley's "Hark! the Herald Angels Sing" dives into what the world might look like if we understood that all of us are within the wide arms of God's grace:

> Hark! the herald angels sing, "Glory to the newborn King;
> peace on *earth*, and mercy mild, God and *sinners* reconciled."
> Joyful, *all* ye nations rise; join the triumph of the skies;
> with the angelic host proclaim, "Christ is born in Bethlehem!"
> Hark! the herald angels sing, "Glory to the newborn King!"[14]
>
> *(emphasis mine)*

This particular hymn seems to crossdenominational lines easier than most, which is surprising when you think of it. The text, originally composed in 1739, was Charles Wesley's response to the popular Calvinist understanding of predestination offered by his good friend and prolific preacher, George Whitefield. Predestination is the belief that, in God's sovereignty, some are elected and chosen for heaven, and others have been preordained for hell. Charles found this understanding to be at odds with his understanding of grace, specifically prevenient grace—the grace of God offered to us before we respond back to God in faith. Charles's poetry nearly borders on a universal understanding of salvation, that God offers salvation to all creation through Christ as the gift that urges us to respond in love of God and love of neighbor. Above, I've highlighted some of the words you may have glossed over when singing this hymn on Sunday mornings, hoping for you to notice the language against Whitefield's Calvinistic preaching. "Peace on earth," not just for some who choose to accept Christ. "God and sinners," not just the elect, are reconciled. And how many nations rise in the triumph of the skies? All.

What if we modeled our Advent and Christmas comings and goings as if we actually believe that God has already blessed everyone?

The year 1739 is an important year in Wesleyan history because it is the year Charles's brother, John Wesley, began his field preaching—that is, preaching outside the walls of the church. Field preaching was offered mainly to the working poor, who were either unable to make it to worship or who were unwelcomed into the sanctuaries. Preaching outside, to the poor, transformed Wesley's understanding of grace, giving rise to sermons like "Free Grace," which begins:

> It is free in all to whom it is given. It does not depend on any power or merit in man; no, not in any degree, neither in whole, nor in part. It does not in anywise depend either on the good works or righteousness of the receiver; not on anything he has done, or anything he is. It does not depend on his endeavors. It does not depend on his good tempers, or good desires, or good purposes and intentions.

Is Tiny Tim's prayer, "God bless us, every one," meant simply to pull at our heartstrings, or can it be a lived reality in our churches and the world? Are we, perhaps, still living in anticipation of "God bless us, every one" becoming a reality? Anticipation and expectation are fundamental to the Christmas experience—it's why we wrap presents and put them under the tree for all to see. There's the anticipation of resolved mystery. *What could it be hidden under the red-and-green wrapping?* There's also the expectation of fulfilled desire. *I hope it's what I want.* Yes, Christmas presents are wrapped in order to conceal, but the box tends to give you a clue about what's inside.

During the Babylonian exile, around six hundred years before Jesus was born, Israel began to anticipate a Messiah. The people held the expectation of an earthly king who would restore the old kingdom in righteousness and truth. The Book of Isaiah records the hope:

> A child is born to us, a son is given to us,
>> and authority will be on his shoulders.
>> He will be named
>> Wonderful Counselor, Mighty God,
>> Eternal Father, Prince of Peace.
> There will be vast authority and endless peace
>> for David's throne and for his kingdom,
>> establishing and sustaining it
>> with justice and righteousness
>> now and forever.
>
> (Isaiah 9:6-7)

They anticipated that God would eventually bring his people out of exile and send them a king. Writing hundreds of years later, even with the knowledge of Jesus' death, Paul echoed this hope in his Letter to the Romans:

> I believe that the present suffering is nothing compared to the coming glory that is going to be revealed to us. The whole creation waits breathless with anticipation for the revelation of God's sons and daughters. Creation was subjected to frustration, not by its own choice—it was the choice of the one who subjected it—but in the hope that the creation itself will be set free from slavery to decay and brought into the glorious freedom of God's children. We know that the whole creation is groaning together and suffering labor pains up until now. And it's not only the creation. We ourselves who have the Spirit as the first crop of the harvest also groan inside as we wait to be adopted and for our bodies to be set free. We were saved in hope. If we see what we hope for, that

isn't hope. Who hopes for what they already see? But if we hope for what we don't see, we wait for it with patience.

(Romans 8:18-25)

The anticipation is palpable. It's as though Israel is a small child sitting at the foot of a Christmas tree just begging to open their presents. The problem is, their anticipation came with a misplaced expectation. In other words, they were sitting at the foot of the tree looking at the wrapped boxes, all the while missing the tree in front of them. Simon Tugwell, in his book *Prayer*, says it well: "If we keep clamouring for things we want from God, we may often find ourselves disappointed, because we have forgotten the weakness of God and what we may call the poverty of God. We had thought of God as the dispenser of all the good things we would possibly desire; but in a very real sense, God has nothing to give at all except himself."[15]

The Christmas story is the story about a miracle.... God decided to put on human flesh so that we could inherit the eternal, a kingdom full of life, built by grace on a foundation of love and justice.

Our Christmas expectations can miss the mark, too. At times our meditations are focused on the boxes rather than on the tree. The Christmas story is the story about a miracle—the infinite and almighty God entered into the world as a helpless baby, born into poverty in an occupied land. God decided to put on human flesh so that we could inherit the eternal, a kingdom full of life, built by grace on a foundation of love and justice.

What are you expecting this Advent and Christmas season? Are you expecting a miracle? The good news is that God has already done the great miracle by sending Jesus to break the bonds of sin and death—that first Christmas was a miracle! And, amazingly, he continues to do miracles by using us—the church, the body of Christ—to make them happen. But too often we get in our own way. Seeing the Cratchits' poverty, Scrooge is moved to pity. He asks the Ghost of Christmas Present if Tiny Tim will be spared, and the spirit answers, "I see a vacant seat . . . in the poor chimney-corner, and a crutch without an owner, carefully preserved. If these shadows remain unaltered by the Future, the child will die" (Stave Three). Scrooge trembles at the thought, pausing only to hear his own words spoken back to him—"If he be like to die, he had better do it, and decrease the surplus population" (Stave Three). Our own misplaced desires and foolishness are a greater enemy to our communion with God than any perceived or real spiritual force of wickedness.

If only we could have been there for the first Nativity. Maybe if we had seen the Christ Child with our own eyes, our Christmas celebrations would be more like what God intends them to be. But the beautiful thing is that we are in the story, in a way. When the shepherds arrived to tell the Holy Family what they had seen and heard from the angels, Luke tells us, "Everyone who heard it was amazed at what the shepherds told them. Mary committed these things to memory and considered them carefully" (Luke 2:18-19). The funny thing is, the only folks present that night were Mary, Joseph, Jesus, and the shepherds, so who is the "everyone" who heard the shepherd's story? We are the "everyone." We should be filled with amazement at their news. We, along with Mary, should treasure and ponder the mystery of God being with us in the flesh. Maybe then Tiny Tim's precious and prophetic prayer will ring true—God has blessed us all, with the gift of himself.

What are you expecting for Christmas this year? Is it something that can be wrapped? It is something that can only be experienced?

What words might the Ghost of Christmas Present say back to you?

How might what you are learning and experiencing this Christmas affect your celebrations in the future?

REFLECTION: LAUGHTER

There is nothing in the world so irresistibly
contagious as laughter and good-humour.
(Stave Three)

Our mouths were suddenly filled with laughter;
*   our tongues were filled with joyful shouts.*
It was even said, at that time, among the nations,
*   "The LORD has done great things for them!"*
Yes, the LORD has done great things for us,
*   and we are overjoyed.*
(Psalm 126:2-3)

In the story of Scrooge, we first see the Ghost of Christmas Present as a happy spirit, with sparkling eyes, a cheery voice, and an unconstrained demeanor. And indeed, when I think about the present, I often think about laughter.

Have you ever burst out laughing at a time when you shouldn't? Not long ago, I was standing at the altar table for

Holy Communion. I took the bread, held it up, and broke it, but before I could speak, a woman's voice rang out from the speakers: "Oh, yes...thank you." There was silence, and then—I'm sorry, God—I had to laugh. The more I tried to hold it back, the more I laughed. Come to find out, our church's formation director had forgotten to mute her microphone after children's worship. She was thanking the children's director for cleaning up the craft room, and apparently a clean craft room is quite important to our formation director!

In Disney's film version of *A Christmas Carol* starring Jim Carrey, the Ghost of Christmas Present has an infectious laugh, because laughter is a great way of commenting on the present. The present simply happens. We can anticipate it, long for it, or maybe want to avoid it, but we can do nothing to stop it. The moment we are aware of what's happening around us, that moment has become part of the past.

One thing I love about laughing is that when we do it, we are rarely self-conscious. We forget about what we're wearing, what we're fighting about, and what's on our to-do list. It's a moment of reckless abandon, which is why laughter reminds me of heaven. I believe that when we rest with God in heaven, God's presence will be felt so strongly that everything else will melt away, including the things that separate us from one another, such as status or creed or fear.

God lives in the present, that moment when we forget the things that hurt our relationships with God and each other. Scripture says, "God is love" (1 John 4:8), and I think laughter offers us a glimpse of God's selfless love that lives within each of us. Laughter erupts because, as the psalmist proclaims, the Lord has done great things for us. After all, what greater gift is there than the Christ Child?

Chapter Four

The Hope of Christmas Future

*He became as good a friend, as good a master, and as good
a man, as the good old city knew. (Stave Five)*

I always get a little tickled when I hear sports analysts try to predict
the outcome of a sporting event. They look at talent levels, statistics
of team achievements, and coaching trends; but at the end of the day,
guessing the winner is simply that—a guess. As far as we have come
with technology, the future is something we still cannot control. The
future is unknown, terribly unpredictable, and awaiting us all. Some
things we do know, or we at least expect. We know that we will not
live forever upon the earth. We expect the sun to rise every morning
and slip below the horizon every night. There are small constants in

our everyday lives, and then there are the larger variables: *Will I find someone to marry? Will I get the job I'm hoping for? Will the test results say "benign"? Will I have enough money to retire?*

The disciples asked Jesus to offer them clues about the future. Jesus said, "You will hear of wars and rumors of wars; see that you are not alarmed...all this is but the beginning of the birth pangs" (Matthew 24:6-8 NRSV). Jesus talked about wars, famines, and earthquakes, but most curiously, Jesus said, "See that you are not alarmed." How can Jesus ask us not to be alarmed about the future? Scrooge was certainly alarmed at what the Ghost of Christmas Yet to Come has to show him, but perhaps we can see in his bleak future some hope for us all.

A GRIM REAPER

"Why do you look for the living among the dead?"
(Luke 24:5)

The happiness Scrooge feels from seeing his friends from the past, and the compassion he feels in hearing Tiny Tim's "God bless us every one," soon gives way to fear, and his journey takes a dark turn. We don't often think about Christmas as a dark time, but Scripture points out that darkness seemed to follow Jesus wherever he went. For instance, Jesus was born during the night. The Gospel of Luke tells us that the shepherds were "guarding their sheep at night" (Luke 2:8). The magi traveled at night, following the Bethlehem star to find the place where Jesus lived as a two-year-old child (see Matthew 2:2). Jesus' father, Joseph, was told in a dream to take his family to Egypt in order to escape Herod's persecution (see Matthew 2:13). Later, during Jesus' ministry, he meets with Nicodemus at night to reveal that one must be born from above (see John 3:2). Before Judas leaves to betray Jesus, Scripture says "and it was night" (John 13:30). Matthew, Mark, and Luke's Gospels tell us that when Jesus was crucified, the sky turned black for hours. Three days later, in John's Gospel, Jesus was resurrected before the sun had risen and later that evening he appeared to the disciples.

Darkness is almost its own character in Jesus' story, and the Ghost of Christmas Yet to Come reminds us of why we should acknowledge the growing darkness of winter days. Last year in the church I serve, we hosted a Christmas healing service to recognize that Christmastime is not a happy time for everyone. Our gathering was simple. We moved the sanctuary chairs in a circle, placed a single candle in the center, sang a song, read some Scripture, and opened the floor for prayer. One woman talked about how her husband had died several months ago, and this was the first Christmas without him. Another person wept, remembering that her father had died on Christmas morning, driving her away from faith in God for many years. Someone who was silent for most of the service surprised us, calling out in a loud voice, "I wish my son could forgive me," before holding her face in her hands. For many, hearing "Merry Christmas" or "Happy Holidays," at the checkout line stings. It is difficult to find healing when we bury our sadness, especially when everyone around us seems to be happy hanging tinsel. That evening we read from Psalm 42:

> My tears have been my food both day and night,
> as people constantly questioned me,
> "Where's your God now?" . . .
> Why, I ask myself, are you so depressed?
> Why are you so upset inside?
> Hope in God!
> Because I will again give him thanks,
> my saving presence and my God.
>
> (Psalm 42:3, 5)

ADVENT WEEK 4: JOY

During the final week of Advent, we light the candle of Joy. By now Christmas is just a few days away. Last-minute shoppers are getting desperate, children are out of school, people are praying that the real Christmas tree they decided to get instead of the fake one in the attic will hold on until Christmas dinner with the family. This close to Christmastime, we can easily become distracted from the joyful anticipation of the coming Christ Child we felt earlier in the year when the Thanksgiving leftovers were still edible.

If you are involved with your worship team, or you are the one fulfilling Christmas lists or preparing a Christmas family meal, it is exceptionally easy to be burning the Advent candles at both ends, so to speak. I remember early in my ministry I volunteered to officiate at the Saturday-night Christmas Eve service at eleven o'clock. I remember getting home in the wee hours of the morning on Christmas Day, grabbing a cup of coffee to help Santa put together a scooter, shutting my eyes for an hour or two, and before I knew it, I was reading the call to worship for Sunday service. When I came home after Sunday worship, I looked at my wife and said, "Whew, I'm tired. What a weekend." She looked back, saying nothing, but I "heard" her loud and clear—*You're tired?!*

It is easy to miss the joy as the calendar moves closer to Christmas, and maybe this is why we light the candle of Joy last. So take a moment, and join me in prayer:

Gracious God, fill us with your joy, the steadfast assurance that you are with us. Help us to remember that this is a holy time, not due to our preparations or celebrations, but because you have chosen to walk among us. In the name of the Father and of the Son and of the Holy Spirit. Amen.

The Psalms give us permission to speak our grievances to God, to shake our fists and ask, "Why?" When—not if—we find ourselves in a dark place, it is important to acknowledge our sadness and talk to God about the heaviness of life. Burying our sadness because we think we are supposed to be happy during Christmas can transform into depression, leaving us with an inability to feel anything at all.

We don't often think about Christmas as a dark time, but Scripture points out that darkness seemed to follow Jesus wherever he went.

After reading the Psalms and listening to one another, I read the Resurrection account in the Gospel of John—"Early in the morning of the first day of the week, while it was still dark, Mary Magdalene came to the tomb and saw that the stone had been taken away from the tomb" (John 20:1). I've always been curious why the stone was removed from the tomb. You would think because Jesus appears to the disciples behind locked doors after the Resurrection, Jesus could have gotten out of the tomb without moving the stone; but seeing the emptiness of the tomb is a very important part of the story.

Scrooge must journey with this Ghost of Christmas Yet to Come into the darkness, not so that he might be scared into changing his life, but so that he can see the emptiness of where his love of money will lead. It may sound odd, but we must see the darkness of the tomb to know that nothing is there. "Why do you look for the living among the dead?" the angels ask the women at the tomb in Luke's Gospel (Luke 24:5). "Looking for the living among the dead" is like thinking that if I had just a bit more, I wouldn't be so depressed. It's like thinking we can bring about salvation through legislation or believing that policy will bring perfection.

It's like the story of Jesus at the wedding in Cana, when he was asked to remedy the embarrassing social *faux pas* of running out of wine before the wedding feast is finished (see John 2:1-11). He noticed six stone jars for purification nearby, and he asked the servants to fill the jars with water to the brim. When the steward drew water from the jars, the water had become wine and the party continued. Hidden within this story is a contradiction. John specifically mentioned there were six jars for purification nearby. The number six often represented imperfection and incompleteness because Creation was completed on the seventh day, when God rested. This, Jesus' first miracle, would have been different if there had been seven stone jars available, because seven often represents completion and perfection. Recording that there were six stone jars for purification is the Gospel's way of poetically expressing how humanity is trying to achieve salvation on its own, trying to find completion on its own terms. Yet Jesus took this imperfection, this lack, and transformed it into the best anyone could have hoped for.

Looking for the living among the dead is like seeking perfection using six stone jars instead of seven. This does not mean that the six stone jars are meaningless—not all legislation is bad, getting a raise isn't evil, and we aren't called to boycott the wedding in Cana because they forgot to put out the seventh jar. It is not that the Resurrection frees us from all earthly concerns; rather Christ was resurrected in the midst of them. Jesus said, "Don't worry about what you will eat" (see Matthew 6:25), not "Don't eat *anything* because I am the Bread of Life." Christ is the light that shines in the darkness. Yes, the darkness is there (hunger, thirst, despair, loneliness), but it is no longer the only thing we can see.

If you have experienced tragedy during the holiday season, it takes a great deal of time for wounds to heal, but they do heal, through patience, prayer, and the humility to ask for help from a loving community. God walks with us through the valley of the darkness (Psalm 23:4), and it is important to acknowledge the darkness and to know that darkness will never be the end of our story. The tomb has a purpose, but its purpose is only understood through its emptiness. In other words, we neither avoid it, nor do we linger there.

Scrooge comes face-to-face with his own finitude. The spirit brings him to his own bedroom, pointing to a body under a still sheet. Dickens writes, "The room was very dark, too dark to be observed with any accuracy, though Scrooge glanced round it in obedience to a secret impulse, anxious to know what kind of room it was. A pale light, rising in the outer air, fell straight upon the bed; and on it, plundered and bereft, unwatched, unwept, uncared for, was the body of this man" (Stave Four). The spirit points to the head of the body, urging Scrooge to pull back the shroud to seemingly gaze upon his own demise. Scrooge admits that he does not have the strength to face himself, and often, neither do we.

I remember meeting once with a young man to hear about his struggle with addiction. He said that when he looked in the mirror he was quick to legitimize his drug use because he thought, *I am only hurting myself. I'm not hurting anyone else.* Then one day he saw his daughter on the floor of the living room, mimicking his drug use. It was then he realized that the decisions he made did, in fact, affect someone other than himself. He said that at that moment the image he saw in the mirror was different. What he saw finally became "true." He admitted that he was an addict and that he needed help. It could be that the spirit wanted Scrooge to see his own face so he could see the truth about who he had become, but Scrooge was not able to take that hard look in the mirror. The spirit then sweeps Scrooge away to see Tiny Tim. Scrooge arrives at the Cratchits' home to notice that the house is quiet and still. He hears someone say, "And he took a child, and set him in the midst of them" (see Mark 9:36 NRSV), and he realizes that Tiny Tim has died. He overhears Bob describe the child's grave to his wife, saying—"I wish you could have gone. It would have done you good to see how green a place it is. But you'll see it often. I promised him that I would walk there on a Sunday. My little, little child!" (Stave Four). Interestingly, after hearing Bob Cratchit's pain and sadness, Scrooge asks the spirit about the man who lay hidden under a shroud in his bed. In a way, the image in the mirror is beginning to change. Scrooge sees that he was invited to dine with the religious elite, and the party began with awkward and prophetic silence.

> One Sabbath, when Jesus went to share a meal in the home of one of the leaders of the Pharisees, they were watching him closely. A man suffering from an abnormal swelling of the body was there. Jesus asked the lawyers and Pharisees, "Does the Law allow healing on the Sabbath or not?" But they said nothing. Jesus took hold of the sick man, cured him, and then let him go. He said to them, "Suppose your child or ox fell into a ditch on the Sabbath day. Wouldn't you immediately pull it out?" But they had no response.
> (Luke 14:1-6)

Scripture says those who invited Jesus to a Sabbath dinner party "were watching him closely." One can imagine suspicious glances and huddled conversations and then, seemingly out of nowhere, a man with dropsy appeared. The man's sudden appearance is no accident—the Pharisees brought the man to Jesus, not so that the poor man might be healed; rather he was inhumanely presented as a means of entrapment. Jesus asked the Pharisees the same question he asked them eight chapters earlier when he healed a man with a withered hand on the Sabbath—"Is it lawful to heal on the Sabbath or not?" except this time Scripture says, "But they had no response" (Luke 14:6). This was the silence of punishment. You can imagine them turning their backs and dismissing Christ with a silence meant to shame and embarrass.

So Jesus met this silence with a miracle. He healed the man and sent him on his way. This healed man reminds us of a different form of silence—the silence of omission. I wonder, what is the man's name? It seems that he is only known by his illness. Time and time again Jesus meets nameless people—a man with dropsy, a woman who is suffering, a man with a withered hand. The sick are not given a name. Often they either aren't given an opportunity to speak, or their words are deemed unimportant and forgotten. They are only remembered because of their faults. Sometimes what is not said in Scripture reveals more than what is said. This form of silence points out apathy, which can be just as damaging. Who around your Christmas tree needs to be heard? Maybe it's the child who no longer wants to sit at the kids' table, but doesn't know how to ask. Maybe it's the person who desperately wants someone to care about how her day is. Maybe it's the person in the kitchen who is tired of being taken for granted. Or maybe it's a person who hasn't yet been invited to the table.

After Jesus healed the man, Jesus continued to probe the Pharisees, saying, "Suppose your child or ox fell into a ditch on the Sabbath day. Wouldn't you immediately pull it out?" (Luke 14:5). This is an appropriate question because dropsy is a disease in which the body fails to process water. The person is constantly thirsty, but the thirst is never quenched. The man was the child drowning in the well, both literally because he was drowning in the water he consumes, but also figuratively because Jesus was trying to get the Pharisees to see him as a child of God, a child in need; but their adherence to the law made them impotent even to do good. Scripture says that the Pharisees were unable to answer—not that they were silent, but that they were unable to answer. This is the silence that exists in the space between disbelief and awe. It is the difference between looking up at the stars and saying, "You are an amazing God," and looking up at the stars to say, "I find no evidence of you." It is the poignant pause on the other end of the phone, waiting to hear either "benign" or "malignant." It is the difference between, "I can't believe what Jesus just did. Let us worship," versus, "I can't believe what Jesus just did. Let's get rid of him." They could not reply because they weren't sure which way to go.

Sometimes silence is unnerving when we are in desperate need of an answer. When we pray to God and "hear" nothing in response, sometimes it leaves us with an uncomfortable and uneasy feeling that God has turned away or that God cannot be bothered with our petitions. I have come to realize that silence is what it sounds like when God is listening. It's not that prayers go unanswered; rather the silence is God's invitation for us to continue speaking. Silence can be punishment. It can be apathy. It can be the space between awe and disbelief. But silence can also be invitation. It can be as simple as truly listening to someone who has something to say. It can be as profound as Christ's silence before Pilate, which invited humanity into the redeeming suffering of the cross.

When Scrooge hears no answer from the spirit, he becomes fearful. Early in Israel's history, recorded in First Samuel, the word of God became rare. Visions were not widespread, God's chosen mediator was riddled with blindness, and a household of priests was perverting its role in the Temple. When Hannah discovered that she was going to have a son, she looked up to the heavens and said, "My heart exults in the LORD; / my strength is exalted in my God.... / He will guard the feet of his faithful ones, / but the wicked shall be cut off in darkness; / for not by might does one prevail. / The LORD will judge the ends of the earth; / he will give strength to his king, / and exalt the power of his anointed." (1 Samuel 2:1, 9-10 NRSV). Little did she know that her son, Samuel, would be the one anointed with the word of God to prepare the way for Israel's greatest king.

The lamp of God had not yet gone out, even though God was silent. The young boy Samuel, dedicated to do the work of God by his mother, was laying down near the ark of God when he heard a voice (see 1 Samuel 3). Twice he heard this voice and twice he ran to Eli, asking if it was he who called, and twice Eli sent the young boy back to sleep. Testament to his apparent blindness, it took three times for Eli to discern that the voice the young child was hearing was the voice of God. Eli told Samuel, "Go, lie down, and if he calls you, answer saying, 'Speak Lord, your servant is listening.'" Not only was Eli blind, but he also was suffering from the despair of uncertainty. "Go, lie down, and IF he calls you... answer." Eli's blindness was affecting more than his eyes—he was uncertain about the future of Israel, the future of his own house, and now, in his own soul, he was uncertain whether God was ever going to speak again.

When Mary, Jesus' mother, visited Elizabeth, John the Baptist's mother, Mary looked up to the heavens and said,

"My soul magnifies the Lord,
    and my spirit rejoices in God my Savior…
His mercy is for those who fear him
    from generation to generation.
He has shown strength with his arm;
    he has scattered the proud in the thoughts of their hearts.
He has brought down the powerful from their thrones,
    and lifted the lowly;
he has filled the hungry with good things,
    and sent the rich away empty.
He has helped his servant Israel,
    in remembrance of his mercy,
according to the promise he made to our ancestors,
    to Abraham and to his descendants forever"

        (Luke 1:46-47, 50-55 NRSV).

Mary's Son was the Word of God, who became the greatest King the world would ever know. Indeed, the word may have been rare, but the lamp of God was not yet extinguished.

Does the word of God seem silent in your heart? Are you caught in a place where your eyes cannot see what tomorrow might bring? Our future may be unknown, but God knows *us* and will hold us.

Does the word of God seem silent in your heart? Are you caught in a place where your eyes cannot see what tomorrow might bring? Our future may be unknown, but God knows *us* and will hold us. "I will let you find me," says the Lord through the prophet Jeremiah (29:14 NRSV). If you are hungry for the light of God, put yourself in a position to hear it. Just as Samuel went to rest in the place where the Spirit of God dwelt, and there heard his voice, Christ calls us to go out and serve those who are hungry, those who are thirsty, those who are in despair, those who are in need of shelter. Christ doesn't call us to provide a handout. Christ calls us to be with the lowly because it is where Christ is and Christ is inviting us to dwell with him. If you are hungry for the light of Christ, then go to where Christ is. God will be there, and if you hear the sound of silence, speak, because God is listening.

Hannah's heart exulted in the Lord, and Mary's soul magnified God's presence. In what ways are you exalting and magnifying what God is doing?

How often do you spend your prayer time in silence? When you do speak, what kind of words do you use when you pray?

How can you stay near the presence of God?

WILL BE, OR MAY BE?

"Answer me one question. Are these the shadows of the things that Will be, or are they shadows of the things that May be, only?" (Stave Four)

We are very near the end of this ghostly Christmas tale, though the ending seems to lack hope. As the Ghost of Christmas Yet to Come points Scrooge toward the grave, he dreadfully asks, "Are these the shadows of the things that Will be, or are they shadows of the things that May be, only?" (Stave Four). Is there any hope left for Scrooge? Can the future be changed, or has God already determined our path? Have you ever considered how much God knows about our future?

There are some things I can only enjoy once: a mediocre football game, *The Da Vinci Code*, an easy puzzle, and so on. For me, experiencing these things for the first time is enough, because when I know the ending or the outcome, these things lose their appeal. I'm no longer invested because the unknown ending was its only offering. Now some things I could experience over and over again, even though I know exactly what is going to happen: a sunset on the beach, *Casablanca*, "Silent Night, Holy Night" on Christmas Eve. I know the ending, but it doesn't dissuade me because these experiences are so much more than just a good ending.

I've always been fascinated by time, especially what we call *the present*. The past is a memory and the future is a dream, but now is what truly exists. The amazing thing about the present is that it is the only moment of which we are aware, but the moment we are aware of it, the moment is in the past. Often during Christmastime we sing "Joy to the World" to celebrate Christ's birth, but this hymn isn't actually about Christ's birth. "Joy to the World," written by prolific poet Isaac Watts in 1719 and based on Psalm 98, details Christ's return at the end of time. The beginning of each of the four stanzas declare,

> Joy to the world! the Lord is come . . .
> Joy to the earth! the Savior reigns . . .
> No more let sin and sorrow grow . . .
> He rules the world with truth and grace . . .[1]

This hymn actually points us to the end of the story rather than the beginning. The Book of Revelation is either spoken of as a book about the past, given to hopeful Christians suffering persecution thousands of years ago, or it is understood as a book only about the future, giving us hints and clues about the end of the world. The author of Revelation, John of Patmos, proclaims that both of these interpretations can miss the point. He writes, "Grace to you and peace from him who *is* and who *was* and who *is to come*" (Revelation 1:4 NRSV, *emphasis mine*). Notice the order of his greeting. He begins with, "Grace to you from him who is." It is profound to read the present tense in a two-thousand-year-old greeting. It's like the angels' proclamation of Jesus' birth to the shepherds in Luke's Gospel. Luke 2 begins with "In *those* days," and "Mary *gave* birth," and "Nearby shepherds *were* living." All of Luke's language is in the past tense. When the angel appears, the language changes to the present. The angel says, "Don't be afraid! Look! I bring good news to you— wonderful, joyous news for all people. Your savior is born today in David's city. He is Christ the Lord" (Luke 2:10-11). Because it is present, it is timeless. "Grace to you from him who *is*." This is the timeless truth that we are not abandoned. In the midst of suffering, we are not alone. God is, and God is with us.

Not only is our God the God of the present, God is also the Lord of the past: "Grace to you from him who *is* and who *was*." God is Lord of the past, which is why forgiveness is possible. Knowing that God is a God of past means that our sins may be forgiven, that God can heal wounds from long ago. When Jesus appeared to Thomas after the Resurrection, interestingly Jesus still had wounds. The wounds had been healed, but the scars were there. The wounds of crucifixion were the worst of humanity, and even these were resurrected and healed.

If God is not a God who *was*, then we who are would never know forgiveness. Not only that, but worshiping a God who *is* and a God who *was* means that our past matters, at least, the goodness you offer today by loving God and loving neighbor, creates a foundation for tomorrow. "I'll seek salvation tomorrow," is not in the Bible. As Paul said in 1 Corinthians 15:1-2, "Brothers and sisters, I want to call your attention to the good news that I preached to you, which you also received and in which you stand. You are being saved through it if you hold on to the message I preached to you, unless somehow you believed it for nothing." Salvation is a process, and it begins today! Did you catch that? "You are *being* saved" (*emphasis mine*) is in the present tense, which means it will always be a present reality. My, how the world would be different if this was our prayer every morning!

Grace to you from him who *is*, and who *was*, and who *is to come*. A God who *is* means that we are not abandoned. A God who *was* means that we are forgiven. A God who *is to come* means that God can be trusted. Several years ago, my wife, Christie, and I had dueling 10:30 a.m. Thanksgiving programs to attend. I started at the day school to see my daughter Annaleigh stand and not sing a word. Then I sneaked out to head over to the elementary school to see my daughter Isabelle's 11 a.m. performance. There are some things Isabelle doesn't care about, but the schedule is not one of them. If we say we are going to the park she wants to know which park, what time we are leaving, and what time we are expecting to leave said park—and woe to the person who deviates from the agreed-upon schedule. So, earlier in the week I told her that I was not going to be in her classroom at 10:30, but that I would meet her on the playground at 11. When I got to the school, three teachers met me on the playground, saying, "Isabelle will certainly be glad to see you." This is teacher code for "there is a problem." I saw her coming from a distance, tears rolling down her face, ponytail all out of whack. I gave her a big hug and said, "I told you I was going to be here. I love you. Don't worry!" A God who is to come is a God whose promise can be trusted.

Scrooge isn't so sure that he wants to see the rest of his story. He shouts to the spirit—

> Hear me! I am not the man I was. I will not be the man I must have been...Why show me this, if I am past all hope!...I will honour Christmas in my heart, and try to keep it all the year. I will live in the Past, the Present, and the Future. The Spirits of all Three shall strive within me. I will not shut out the lessons that they teach. (Stave Four)

Scrooge's past made him who he was. If you do, in fact, reap what you sow, Scrooge's story will not end well. Scrooge asks whether seeing his future demise is a vision of what will be or what may be. It's an interesting question to think about but will an answer to his question ultimately matter? Scripture tells us everything we need to know, but it doesn't tell us everything we want to know.

Through faith in Christ, our present, our past, and our future are held together in grace.

One day a rich young ruler asks Jesus what he must do to inherit eternal life. Jesus tells him to go, sell all that he owns, give to the poor, and follow him. The man walks away full of sorrow; but we don't know whether he walks away sad because he's about to sell all of his possessions so that he can follow Jesus, or whether he is sad because he loves his possessions too much to follow Jesus. The father who had two sons in Jesus' famous prodigal son story threw a party for the younger brother, but what happened the next morning? Did he then shower the faithful older son with lavish gifts? Scripture doesn't tell us everything we want to know, but it does tell us everything we need to know, and all we need to know is no matter the past and no matter what the future holds, God is with us now and wants nothing more than to be with us.

What are God's promises? Revelation says, "To the one who loves us and freed us from our sins by his blood, who made us a kingdom, priests to his God and Father—to him be glory and power forever and always" (Revelation 1:5b-6). Pay close attention to the tense within the passage. "To the one who loves us" is in the present tense. This is the promise of the God who is. "And freed us from our sins," is in the past tense. This is the promise of the God who was. "And made us a kingdom" is pointing us toward the future. This is the work of the God who is to come. God loves us, has forgiven us, and has given us purpose for the future, beginning today as servants to God and for each other. Through faith in Christ, our present, our past, and our future are held together in grace.

What story from Scripture leaves you scratching your head, wanting to know more?

What does it mean to you that God is, was, and is to come?

CAROL OF THE BELLS

"It's Christmas Day!" said Scrooge to himself. "I haven't missed it." (Stave Five)

Early in the morning Scrooge wakes up from the strangest dream he's ever had. He opens the window and discovers that it is Christmas morning, and he has been given a chance to change his ways. He did nothing to earn it; rather it was a gift. He shouts to himself, "I am as light as a feather, I am as happy as an angel. I am as merry as a schoolboy. I am as giddy as a drunken man. A merry Christmas to everybody! A happy New Year to all the world. Hallo here! Whoop! Hallo!" (Stave Five).

Scrooge's joy reminds me of the year we got our daughter Isabelle a gift that she didn't even know she wanted. Isabelle is a huge fan of the Legend of Zelda videogame franchise, so we got her tickets to the Symphony of the Goddess, a concert of Legend of Zelda music set to visual scenes from the video game. She certainly felt "light as a feather" when she saw the tickets. Have you been given anything you didn't know you wanted or needed, but loved? Gift-giving at its best is a present for which we didn't ask, and didn't think we needed, but reveals that the gift-giver really knows us. This is why we celebrate Jesus as a gift during the Christmas season.

The Christmas story is a story in three scenes. *Scene 1*. The curtain opens and we see a magnificent palace, the seat of human power and authority. Caesar sits on his throne and commands that the entire world is to be counted. The news of Caesar's census travels to Quirinius, governor of Syria, lower than Caesar in influence but powerful enough to be remembered by name. Joseph and Mary enter the scene, preparing to make the journey from Nazareth in the north to Bethlehem in the south so that the proper authorities may count them. While they are in Bethlehem, the time comes for Mary to deliver her child. She gives birth to a baby boy, wraps him in bands of cloth, and places him in a manger because there is no room for them in the inn.

The scene begins at the palace and ends with no place. It begins with Caesar, who was named emperor of the world, and ends with a baby placed in a feeding trough. It begins with the seat of human power and ends with those who live in powerless poverty. It begins with everyone being counted and ends with a baby revealing that everyone counts. God is beginning to turn the world upside down for all of the right reasons.

Scene 2. We find ourselves on the outskirts of town, where the third-shift shepherds scan the darkness surrounding the fold for any sign of danger. Then an angel of the Lord stands before them and they are afraid. Their job was to protect the herd from danger, and now standing before them is a potential threat they have never seen, which is why the angel first said, "Don't be afraid." Some have asked why we light the candle of Peace before hope, and it is because it is difficult to hear hopeful news in the midst of fear. Do not be afraid. Peace be with you. Hear the good news of great joy. The Messiah is born! Then the angel said something curious—"This is a sign for you: you will find a newborn baby wrapped snugly and lying in a manger" (Luke 2:12). The wise men receive the sign of a star, but the shepherds needed something a bit more practical—they needed a manger, a feeding trough for animals. They knew how to find a manger.

God speaks to us in a language we can hear and understand. The magi had a star. The shepherds were offered a manger. How is God speaking with you? It may be frightening at first, because an encounter with God turns things on its head; but don't be afraid. This is a story of great joy—the steadfast assurance that God is with us. The shepherds said, "Let's go to Bethlehem—now," or as Billy Crystal said to Meg Ryan in *When Harry Met Sally*, "when you realize you want to spend the rest of your life with someone, you want the rest of your life to start as soon as possible."[2]

Scene 3. The curtain opens on the shepherds having found the child lying in a manger, and they tell the Holy Family all that has happened. They can't offer treasures of gold, frankincense, or myrrh, and yet Mary treasures the gift they did offer—their words—in her heart. The shepherds do not linger. They return to the fields, but they returned forever changed.

In each scene of our three-scene story, there is only one image continued throughout—the manger. In the first scene the child is placed in the manger. In the second scene the angel proclaims that the manger will be a sign to them. In the third scene the manger is found and celebrated. It's like God is setting the Holy Communion table long before we hear of the Last Supper. The manger is the sign that God is beginning to redeem God's people, and the child wrapped in swaddling clothes is the one from whom we will forever find our nourishment. Maybe this is why the first thing Scrooge does on Christmas morning is to buy the largest turkey at the poulterer's for the Cratchits. He heard Bob say, "Have you ever seen such a goose," and in Scrooge's own way, he wants Bob's hope to come into fruition.

Even though theological words are rather absent from Dickens's story, *redemption* is a word that both Scrooge and churchgoer recognize.

Scrooge has been redeemed. Even though theological words are rather absent from Dickens's story, *redemption* is a word that both Scrooge and churchgoer recognize. Redemption means exchange—something is offered, and something is received. It's like when you redeem a coupon in a store. You present a coupon for 10 percent off, and you receive 10 percent back from your bill's total. When we talk about redemption in the church, the picture we sometimes present is that redemption means we give our heart to Christ, and God rewards us with salvation, or heaven, like giving a coupon and getting a discount. A more accurate picture is, God has already offered us salvation, and responding to that gift is where transformation takes place. The Letter to the Ephesians says, "We have been ransomed through his Son's blood, and we have forgiveness for our failures based on his overflowing grace" (Ephesians 1:7). Later in the letter the author says, "You are saved by God's grace because of your faith" (Ephesians 2:8). Salvation has already been offered, and our goal is to respond to God's grace. We are the redeemed, and our response to that redemption reveals our commitment to God's grace, love, and mercy. Scrooge certainly did not earn a new day, but he responds to this gift well.

You might wonder why someone like Scrooge is offered a new day. He's not a young man with thirty years of philanthropy ahead.

If "you reap what you sow" is correct, he probably doesn't have time to make up for all of the pain he has caused. Scrooge reminds me of Lazarus, Jesus' dear friend whom Jesus brings back from the dead in John 11. Jesus commanded Lazarus to come out of the tomb, and surprising everyone, he does! Why would Jesus raise Lazarus only for Lazarus to die again one day? Why would Scrooge be offered another day when presumably his life is nearly over? Of course, Lazarus coming back from the dead is an important story, and one that foreshadows Jesus' own resurrection; but the point is what Jesus said while Lazarus is lumbering into the light. As Lazarus slowly exited the tomb, Christ commanded him to be unbound.

Scrooge is now "unbound," so to speak. He has not been given a new day in order to make amends; rather he has been given a new day in order to experience an unbound joy. Through his lack of compassion and empathy, Scrooge had become a shell of a person. He had forgotten who he was. Interestingly, this is the Scrooge we can't forget. It would sound odd to greet a happy caroler at your door saying, "What a delightful Scrooge that child was." Maybe, after it all, the point of *A Christmas Carol* is not to see how Scrooge is transformed, but to understand "you reap what you sow" in a different, more graceful, way. Otherwise, in our own mind, Scrooge will never find true redemption. We will continue to live as if the bad will always outweigh the good.

Perhaps Scrooge was meant to remind us of . . . the heart of the gospel itself: the lost sheep did not find its way back into the fold; rather it was found.

Perhaps Scrooge was meant to remind us of the heart of Luke 15, and the heart of the gospel itself: the lost sheep did not find its way back into the fold; rather it was found. The lost coin did not jump back into the woman's purse. She searched for it. The prodigal son did not earn his way back into his father's house. The father embraced his return. In all three parables, the community is asked to do one thing—rejoice. Rejoice with me that the sheep is found. Rejoice with me that the coin is found. Rejoice with me that my son, who was dead, is alive. Our job in the story is to rejoice over what God is doing in the person of Christ. "I bring good news to you—wonderful, joyous news for all people," the angel said to the shepherds (Luke 2:10). When we find joy—the steadfast assurance that God is with us, we will recognize the redemption the Christ Child was born to offer, and we will celebrate Scrooge's rebirth rather than remember his faults. As Christians we are to live unbound lives, which means we do not play by the rules of the world. So maybe it's time for us to start a new tradition—to give new meaning to Scrooge's own name.

Why do you suppose we are so quick to perpetuate the idea of the Scrooge before his transformation?

How do you understand "You reap what you sow"? Could there be a more graceful understanding of that passage?

How might you encourage others to be "unbound" as followers of Christ?

KEEP CHRISTMAS WELL

It was always said of him, that he knew how to keep Christmas well, if any man alive possessed the knowledge.
(Stave Five)

Before hearing the famous, "God bless us, every one," at the end of Dickens's classic story, we hear that Scrooge learned how to "keep Christmas well." I wonder if the same would be said of us. How do we keep Christmas well? Maybe the entire point of *A Christmas Carol* lies in three small words: *keep Christmas well.*

What are we called to "keep"? I remember when I first moved to The Well United Methodist Church, to follow the founding pastor. The leadership team offered me two rules of success—I was not to wear a tie (because worship was very casual in style), and they don't like anything traditional (because both worship services were "contemporary"). I accepted their challenge. I've never been a fan of wearing ties anyway. The worship team was gracious in letting me stretch the congregation musically, going so far as to host a "Whocharist" (a Communion service using only music by The Who to tell Jesus' story), until we began planning Advent. After spending some time developing a seasonal theme, I was handed a list of the church's Christmas songs. I took the list, made a few changes, and then sent it out to the worship team. It didn't take me long to feel the tension during band practice later that week. The community was gracious and hospitable toward changing things up in September, but the closer we came to the holy time of Christmas, change was no longer an exciting symptom of having a new pastor (note to new pastors: don't change anything until Jesus is born, and then don't change anything until Jesus has been raised. Keep these two, and you will do well). At that time, the congregation was five years old, and there already was an expectation for what Christmas worship was supposed to be. The nontraditional church still expected to sing a candlelit "Silent Night, Holy Night" before the Christmas Eve benediction. In other words, typically when a congregation says it is nontraditional, what they really mean to say is that our tradition is different. At least, rarely have I experienced a Christian community who likes to change things up every year on Christmas Eve.

So what do we *keep* and how do we *keep* it? Keeping tradition helps us feel rooted, and often surrounds us with a non-anxious familiar presence. Even if we feel our tradition is different, it tends to be consistently different in the same way. Christmas is a precious time, but if we are honest, it's not any more or less precious than any other day the Lord has made. On the one hand we are in love with meeting expectations. If something last year filled us with happiness, we want to reproduce it to ensure a joyful experience. On the other hand, if your friend was excited that he found the latest gadget in his stocking last year, opening the same gift again this year would miss the point.

Sometimes what we keep fails to meet expectations because it feels lifeless, boring, or stale (only fruitcake doesn't spoil, and even then it should never be a gift). The Advent candles remind us what we are called to keep during the holiday season. We should keep Peace, continually learning how to love our enemy and break bread with the outcast and forgotten. We should keep Hope, always trusting in God for the goodness we yet do not see in the world. We should keep Love because God is love (1 John 4:8), and God is calling us to share God's presence with the world. We should keep Joy, constantly remembering the steadfast assurance that God is with us. We do not have to keep the same level of gift-giving debt, which leaves the offering plates bare come January. We do not have to keep the fear and anxiety of creating the perfect Christmas. We do not have to keep the same invitation list to the white elephant party, which excluded the family member with whom you were fighting. We are called to keep the Scriptures and the truth within them. Everything else can be nailed to the cross come Good Friday.

What we "keep" applies to our everyday life with God, but what about the Christmas tree, stockings, carols, and candlelit "Silent Night, Holy Night"? How do we "keep" Christmastime? I will admit that I've tried to sing Christmas carols during July, and it doesn't work. Christmas is a special time of year, and that's okay! Keeping Christmas means to get lost in the angel's ever-present announcement that Christ is born. Keeping Christmas means that when the days get darker we light the way to our homes and churches. Keeping

Christmas means we do spend extra time with the choir and band starting in October to ensure the most beautiful and exciting music we can muster. Keeping Christmas means we do adorn our sanctuaries with evergreen to remind ourselves that God's story is about life when little seems life-giving out there. We are called to keep Christmas by not shying away from saying, "Merry Christmas," while also not chastising or feeling threatened by a "Happy Holidays." Can we offer an honest, "thank you," when someone is nice enough to wish us well? We keep Christ in Christmas not through bumper stickers or anger toward coffee cups or making sure city hall has the largest Christmas tree; rather Christ is with us in our invitation, in our selflessness, our service, and our humble witness. If there is a war on Christmas, it is a civil war between those who embody "O come let us adore him," and those who are upset that the angels didn't make their prophetic announcement in a department store.

**We are called to *keep*,
we are called to *keep Christmas*,
and we are called to *keep Christmas well*.**

We are called to *keep*, we are called to *keep Christmas*, and we are called to *keep Christmas well*. The Ghosts of Christmas Past, Present, and Yet to Come certainly aided Scrooge in discovering how to keep Christmas well. The compassion he found for Tiny Tim and Bob Cratchit stirred Scrooge's soul. Reliving the joy of seeing Mr. and Mrs. Fezziwig twirl about brought a smile to his rigid and timeworn face. Offering donations and gifts to the community was the fruit of Scrooge's redemption, revealing that he was a new and joyful person. As beautiful and important as these experiences are, I am convinced that Scrooge doesn't know how to keep Christmas well until he allows his nephew, Fred, to welcome and receive him. Earlier in the story Fred offers Scrooge a Christmas dinner invitation, but he wants to be left alone. "Keep Christmas in your own way, and let me keep it in mine," he replies (Stave One). After his nephew presses the crotchety miser, Scrooge dismisses him altogether with the less than genuine and stubbornly repeated phrase, "Good afternoon!" At the end of the story, Scrooge knows what he must do. His journey will not be complete until he humbly and selflessly reconciles with his family. He approaches Fred's door, a home he walked past dozens of times without the courage to knock. He wanders into the dining room and says, "I have come to dinner. Will you let me in, Fred?" (Stave Five). Fred welcomes him to dinner exuberantly, and a wonderful party ensues.

Christmas is...a gift from God, calling us to respond in the world with love.

When the invitation is accepted, Scrooge's redemptive journey is complete. Christmas is an invitation into relationship with God, through Christ, in the power of the Holy Spirit. Christ is born so that God might have ears to hear our wants, eyes to see our need, hands to outstretch on the cross in order to clothe us in his resurrection, and lips to speak the story of good news, that we might share with the world. When Christ's invitation is accepted, we discover that we have been redeemed. We have neither earned it nor do we deserve it. It is a gift from God, calling us to respond in the world with love. Scrooge knocked at the door and asked to be welcomed, and with joy, he was. If Scrooge can be redeemed, then so can we!

How will you "keep" Christmas this year? What new traditions might you adopt?

What invitation do you need to offer to someone? Which invitation do you need to accept?

REFLECTION: A NEW DAY

*"I am as light as a feather, I am as happy as
an angel, I am as merry as a schoolboy. I am as
giddy as a drunken man. A merry Christmas to
everybody! A happy New Year to all the world!"*

(Stave Five)

*Then I saw a new heaven and a new earth, for
the former heaven and the former earth had
passed away, and the sea was no more.*

(Revelation 21:1)

I will admit that I am a bit of a music snob. I spend too much time selecting the songs for worship, because they have to be perfect—easy to sing, musically interesting, theologically correct, and seasonally appropriate. I rarely like any music I didn't personally discover, and it drives my wife, Christie, bonkers!

138

For months Christie had been recommending Mindy Smith's latest Christmas album, but I was too busy trying to figure out how Alison Krauss and Yo-Yo Ma's "Wexford Carol" might work in a contemporary setting. One afternoon while decorating the house for a Christmas gathering, Christie played Mindy Smith's "Away in a Manger" in the background. Smith uses the alternate melody to the song, the one that many Protestants are not familiar with. I stopped what I was doing, and our conversation went something like this:

"Who is this? This is great!"

"The artist I've been trying to get you to listen to for months."

"I like it."

"I knew you would!"

Christie knows me well. She also knows that sometimes you have to experience things on your own terms for them to make a lasting impression.

This is the journey Scrooge had to take. When he woke up on Christmas morning, everything looked different. Earlier in his story, the streets had been dim and the weather frightful. Now he overflowed with happiness and found that "everything could yield him pleasure" (Stave Five).

Now that you are finishing *The Redemption of Scrooge*, what looks different to you? How might you share *A Christmas Carol* in your own words? How could you share the Nativity story in your own context? Is your understanding of God's redemptive gift in the person of Christ a little more fruitful?

If not, that's okay. At the end of God's story, the Book of Revelation, we hear that there will be a new heaven and a new earth. In other words, one day even our longest-standing Christmas traditions will all be made new. This reminds me that whether we are right or wrong, whether we preserve our Christmas traditions or keep searching for something new, whether we are more like Scrooge than we care to admit, God offers us a new day. I pray that you might see that this new day begins today.

Gracious God, you who make all things new, renew us this day and every day, so that we might be strengthened by the power of the Holy Spirit to reach out in love and service to the world. Amen.

ACKNOWLEDGMENTS

I am so thankful to share this study with you, but this study would not have happened without some very special people. I first have to thank my wife, Christie, and my amazing children Isabelle, Annaleigh, Cecilia, and Robert for sharing me with the ministry in general and this study in particular. I have to especially thank The Well United Methodist Church for offering me the grace to always be writing, and Asbury United Methodist Church for welcoming me into this next ministry chapter. I want to offer a huge shout out to "The Scripted Yeahs" (The Well worship band) for having more fun in worship than anyone thought possible: Billy Takewell, Ben Thomas, Wade Hymel, Cody Coulon, Heather Sullivan, David Gambino, Rebecca Gambino, Melissa Durand, Royce Pardue, and Craig McGehee.

I must also lift up my colleagues in ministry who have challenged and supported me: Rev. (Obi-wan) Ken Irby, Rev. James C. Howell, Rev. Justin Coleman, and Dr. David Hobson. Thank you to Scrooge himself, Mark Price, for your inspiration and expertise. I also want to acknowledge the support of my colleagues in the Louisiana Conference of The United Methodist Church.

I am so thankful to Abingdon Press for offering me this opportunity. To the team: Susan Salley, Ron Kidd, Alan Vermilye, Tim Cobb, Marcia Myatt, Tracey Craddock, Camilla Myers, Sally Sharpe, and Sonia Worsham. I also must lift up Lori Jones for making me sound better than I deserve—you have a gift, my friend.

NOTES

INTRODUCTION

1. *Merriam-Webster Online*, s. v., "carol," accessed April 27, 2016, http://www.merriam-webster.com/dictionary/carol.

CHAPTER ONE: BAH! HUMBUG!

1. "Ebenezer," British Baby Names, http://www.britishbabynames.com/blog/2015/02/ebenezer.html.
2. "Come, Thou Fount of Every Blessing," words by Robert Robinson (1758), *The United Methodist Hymnal* (Nashville: The United Methodist Publishing House, 1989), 400.
3. *Latdict*, s. v., "venire," accessed April 27, 2016, http://www.latin-dictionary.net/search/latin/venire.
4. "On Christmas Carols" in *The Beauties of the Magazines, and Other Periodical Works, Selected for a Series of Years*, vol. 2 (1775), printed for Gottlob Emanuel Richter, https://books.google.ch/books?id=RyAVAAAAQAAJ&pg=PA87#v=onepage&q&f=false 87f.
5. William Sandys, *Christmas Carols, Ancient and Modern; Including the Most Popular in the West of England, and the Airs which They Sung* (London: Forgotten Books, 2015), eBook.
6. "God Rest You Merry, Gentlemen," http://www.gbod3.org/musicdownloads/GodRestYouMerryGentlemen.pdf.
7. Michael Schneider, "How The Goldbergs and Other New Shows Kept Their Theme Songs," *TV Guide*, November 1, 2013, http://www.tvguide.com/news/new-show-theme-songs-1072874/. See also http://dragonet.wikidot.com/rewind.

CHAPTER TWO: THE REMEMBERANCE OF CHRISTMAS PAST

1. *Monty Python's Flying Circus*, Season 1, Episode 2.
2. Stanley Hauerwas, *Matthew* (*Brazos Theological Commentary on the Bible*) (Grand Rapids, MI: Brazos Press, 2015), 35.
3. Gregory of Nazianzus, Epistle 101.

CHAPTER THREE: THE LIFE OF CHRISTMAS PRESENT

1. "Love Came Down at Christmas," Christina Georgina Rossetti, 1885, http://www.hymnary.org/text/love_came_down_at_christmas.

2. "The Nicene Creed," *The United Methodist Hymnal* (Nashville: The United Methodist Publishing House, 1989), 880.

3. Shane Claiborne, Jonathan Wilson-Hartgrove, Enuma Okoro, *Common Prayer: A Liturgy for Ordinary Radicals* (Grand Rapids, MI: Zondervan, 2010), 178.

4. Mike Slaughter, *Christmas Is Not Your Birthday*, (Nashville: Abingdon Press, 2011).

5. "Silent Night, Holy Night," words by Joseph Mohr and music by Franz Gruber (1818), *The United Methodist Hymnal* (Nashville: The United Methodist Publishing House, 1989), 239, stanza 3.

6. Scott Bader-Saye, *Following Jesus in a Culture of Fear: The Christian Practice of Everyday Life*, (Grand Rapids, MI: Brazos Press, 2007), 51.

7. Ibid., 66.

8. "O Little Town of Bethlehem," words by Philips Brooks and music by Lewis Redner (1868), *The United Methodist Hymnal* (Nashville: The United Methodist Publishing House, 1989), 230, stanza 1.

9. "Bethlehem," http://www.biblestudytools.com/dictionary /bethlehem/.

10. "Nazareth," http://www.biblestudytools.com/dictionary/nazareth/.

11. "Jerusalem," http://www.biblestudytools.com/dictionary/jerusalem/.

12. Samuel Wells, *A Nazareth Manifesto: Being With God* (Hoboken, NJ: Wiley, 2015), 29.

13. John Wesley, "Free Grace" (Sermon 128), The United Methodist Church, http://www.umcmission.org/Find-Resources /John-Wesley-Sermons/Sermon-128-Free-Grace.

14. "Hark! the Herald Angels Sing," Charles Wesley, 1739, edited by George Whitefield in 1753, http://www.hymnary.org/text /hark_the_herald_angels_sing_glory_to.

15. Quoted in Rueben Job and Norman Shawchuck, *A Guide to Prayer for Ministers and Other Servants* (Nashville: The Upper Room, 1983), 250.

CHAPTER FOUR: THE HOPE OF CHRISTMAS FUTURE

1. "Joy to the World," Isaac Watts (1719), http://www.hymnary.org /text/joy_to_the_world_the_lord_is_come.

2. *"When Harry Met Sally...* Quotes," IMDb, http://www.imdb.com /title/tt0098635/quotes.